Lex Aeterna

Lex Aeterna

A Defense of the Orthodox Lutheran Doctrine of God's
Law and Critique of Gerhard Forde

JORDAN COOPER

WIPF & STOCK · Eugene, Oregon

LEX AETERNA
A Defense of the Orthodox Lutheran Doctrine of God's Law and Critique of Gerhard Forde

Copyright © 2017 Jordan Cooper. All rights reserved. Except for brief quotations in critical publications or reviews, no part of this book may be reproduced in any manner without prior written permission from the publisher. Write: Permissions, Wipf and Stock Publishers, 199 W. 8th Ave., Suite 3, Eugene, OR 97401.

Wipf & Stock
An Imprint of Wipf and Stock Publishers
199 W. 8th Ave., Suite 3
Eugene, OR 97401

www.wipfandstock.com

PAPERBACK ISBN: 978-1-5326-1635-8
HARDCOVER ISBN: 978-1-4982-4009-3
EBOOK ISBN: 978-1-4982-4008-6

Manufactured in the U.S.A.   JANUARY 20, 2017

To Joel Biermann,
whose teaching on the law and the two kinds of righteousness has helped form my own pastoral ministry and writing on this subject.

Contents

1. Introduction | 1
2. Literature Review | 8
3. The Scriptural and Theological Foundations for the Distinction between Law and Gospel in Confessional Lutheranism | 41
4. The Distinction between Law and Gospel in the Theology of Gerhard Forde Compared and Contrasted with Confessional Lutheranism | 79
5. Conclusion: Implications of the Dissonance between Gerhard Forde and Confessional Lutheranism | 110

Bibliography | *149*

1

Introduction

Background

THE DISTINCTION BETWEEN THE law and the gospel is at the heart of Lutheran Reformational theology.[1] Due to this fact, there have been several debates in Lutheran history surrounding the correct understanding of these two concepts. Already among the second-generation Reformers, a debate began surrounding the third use of the law in the Christian life. This was settled in Article VI of the Formula of Concord. The debates regarding the third use of the law and the relationship between God's commands and his promises did not end in 1580, however. Within the last hundred years, there has been a broad discussion relating to the Lutheran law-gospel paradigm.

In this work, it is contended that the shifts which have occurred in the theological world regarding law and gospel lead to a number of problems in expositing the doctrine of the divine law. In modern Lutheran theology, the eternal nature of God's law has been neglected, and in many places, rejected outright. This has led to a radical revision of the entire theological enterprise from a Lutheran perspective. For this reason, many critiques of the Lutheran tradition rely on a caricature of historical views, rather than a careful exposition of the theological categories inherent in historic Lutheranism. I contend, in contrast to these contemporary movements, that the recovery of the traditional Lutheran approach to the law is a beneficial, and necessary, move for the modern church. Not only is this understanding of the law necessary for the Lutheran church, but the insights of historic

1. This work is an edited version of a Master's thesis written for the South African Theological Seminary. It is used with permission.

Lutheran theologians regarding this topic can be immensely beneficial for the church catholic. Recovering those insights would also allow the church to open up dialogue between theological traditions which have often viewed the Lutheran Reformation with suspicion due to its seeming antinomianism and disparagement of the goodness of God's law.

The contemporary debates surrounding the distinction between law and gospel in Lutheranism are perhaps exemplified within the writings of German theologian Werner Elert. In various writings, especially his monumental work *The Structure of Lutheranism* (1962), Elert expounds upon the distinction between law and gospel in largely existential categories.[2] In opposition to Barth's reversal of the law-gospel distinction, Elert argues that law always precedes gospel. God's word of command follows his word of promise.[3] Yet, Elert defines the law primarily in relation to its effect upon the one hearing it. In this way, the law and condemnation became almost synonymous concepts. Elert denies the traditional confessional teaching regarding the third use of the law, viewing it as a Reformed invention which wrongfully infiltrated Lutheranism through Philip Melanchthon.

Among those who follow within the existential Lutheran tradition is Gerhard Forde. In his doctoral dissertation, published as *The Law-Gospel Debate* (1969), Forde traces the debates surrounding law and gospel and the third use of the law from the late nineteenth- through the mid-twentieth centuries. Though critical of Elert on a number of points, Forde adopts his rejection of the third use of the law, and similarly defines law by its effects upon the hearer. Forde expounded upon these ideas in a number of books and essays throughout his career. In *Justification by Faith: A Matter of Death and Life* (1990), Forde places the doctrine of justification within a death-life paradigm. This death-life distinction is, for Forde, synonymous with the distinction between law and gospel. In defining the traditional Lutheran paradigm in such a manner, Forde rejects the formulations of Lutheran scholasticism and the later confessional documents. This redefinition of law and gospel is also apparent in the manner in which he treats the subject of atonement in *Where God Meets Man* (1972) and other writings. In this work, Forde contends that Jesus does not obey the law on behalf of

---

2. This is not to say that Elert heavily cites Heidegger or other existential philosophers in the sense that Bultmann does. His existentialism lies in his emphasis on a thing's effects upon an individual, rather than their actual essence or content. This is especially true in relation to the law and the gospel.

3. Barth, "Gospel and Law." See also John Hesselink's overview of this debate in "Law and Gospel or Gospel and Law? Karl Barth, Martin Luther, and John Calvin."

humanity, because salvation would then remain in the hands of the law rather than the gospel. Forde discusses these and other issues in his chapters on justification and the Christian life in *Christian Dogmatics*.[4] In this work, Forde clearly outlines his opposition to the third use of the law as explained in the Formula of Concord.

David Scaer, in his book *Law and Gospel and the Means of Grace* (2008), gives what is likely the most detailed discussion of the distinction between law and gospel from a contemporary confessional Lutheran perspective. Scaer maintains that in the Lutheran Confessions, the phrase "law and gospel" does often refer to God's act of condemning and redeeming.[5] This is not, however, the *only* way in which this formula is used. Scaer contends for the goodness of both the law and the gospel and argues that the law serves a positive function within the Christian life alongside its condemnatory use. Through an evaluation of twentieth-century Lutheran perspectives, Scaer rejects Elert's denial of the third use as opposed to the Lutheran Confessions and Scripture.

Joel Biermann, in his book *A Case for Character: Towards a Lutheran Virtue Ethics* (2014), argues that the law-gospel paradigm has been wrongly utilized in much of contemporary Lutheran theology. He argues that a balanced approach to law and gospel has been replaced by law-gospel reductionism. In historic Lutheranism, the law and the gospel are viewed as distinct, but they are not contradictory. Yet, in the writings of some contemporary Lutheran figures like Gerhard Forde, these two words of God are viewed as a polarity; they contradict one another. Biermann alleges that this has led to the neglect of ethical discourse from the Lutheran pulpit. He argues that while the law-gospel paradigm remains essential for Lutheran theology and life, it is not exhaustive of biblical teaching. Biermann proposes another paradigm, which he labels "the three kinds of righteousness," as a supplementary teaching to the traditional Lutheran law-gospel dichotomy. In this model, there is a distinction between righteousness *coram mundo* and righteousness *coram Deo*. Before God, the law condemns; before the world, it serves as a guide for the believer to follow. Thus, the law is a good gift of God, and though it accuses and kills, it does not *only* serve in this function.

There is a clear disparity between two views within Lutheran literature in the late twentieth and early twenty-first centuries. There is one tradition,

---

4. Braaten, *Christian Dogmatics* 2:391–469.
5. Scaer, *Law and Gospel*, 3.

beginning with Elert, and exemplified in the writings of Gerhard Forde, which identifies the law and the gospel almost exclusively with existential realities. In contrast to this, several writers within the confessional Lutheran tradition, including David Scaer and Joel Biermann, have sought to recapture the importance of the traditional law-gospel paradigm. In this traditional schema, the law and the gospel refer to objective realities relating to God's commands and promises. The third use of the law is thus a true and beneficial aspect of Christian, and particularly Lutheran, theology.

Problem and Objectives

The central premise of this work is that the Radical Lutheran movement, exemplified by the theology of Gerhard Forde, is not consistent with confessional Lutheranism, and that a historic understanding of the law must be recovered. Gerhard Forde, in his 1987 article "Radical Lutheranism," proposes that the Lutheran church must move forward by holding to a radical conception of the doctrine of justification.[6] He does this through an emphasis on the law as an instrument of death and the gospel as an instrument of life. This present work seeks to demonstrate that Forde's central thesis is incompatible with the confessions because Forde argues for an approach to law and gospel (and consequently justification) which is based upon existential encounter rather than objective theological content. In opposition to Forde's approach, a positive treatment of the law is explained in order to reestablish a traditional understanding of the distinction between law and gospel within Lutheranism.

Each figure within the broader Radical Lutheran movement has his or her own particular perspective. It would be impossible for a study of this size to scrutinize each figure extensively. Thus, this study is limited to the thought of Gerhard Forde. Other writers in the movement will be cited, but only insofar as they repeat or influence the doctrines of Forde. This study is also limited in its scope in reference to Forde's theology. The redefinition of the law in Forde's thought has implications for his approach to sanctification, worship, the doctrine of God, and many other doctrines. These ideas will only be touched on incidentally, however, so that the study can be more narrowly focused on the definition of law and gospel and the use of such a distinction. This study applies beyond the work of Forde himself, as he is simply representative of a broader theological tradition. Thus, readers

---

6. Forde, "Radical Lutheranism," 7, found in Forde, *Radical Gospel*.

unfamiliar with the particularities of Forde's own thought will still benefit from reading this text.

Throughout this work, the contention is made that the views of Forde and the tradition following his views is incommensurate with the confessional tradition. The essential difference between Forde and the confessions is that Forde defines both the law and the gospel by their *effects* rather than their *content*. He uses law and gospel in reference to the *opera Dei* (works of God), whereas confessional Lutheranism describes law and gospel as the *verba Dei* (words of God). He argues that "The law is defined not only as a specific set of demands as such, but rather in terms of what it does to you."[7] Because of his approach to the law as that which kills, there is no positive function for the law in the Christian life for Forde. Lutheran orthodoxy, in contrast, asserts that the law is the eternal will of God.[8] Because of their divergent views of the law, the definitions of the gospel in Forde and confessional Lutheranism differ. According to Forde, "the gospel too, is defined primarily by what it does: the gospel comforts because it puts an end to the voice of the law."[9] In contrast, the Lutheran Confessions define the gospel with specific doctrinal content. The Formula of Concord identifies the gospel with the objective historical actions of Christ in history on behalf of sinners. This includes Christ's active obedience to the law and his passive vicarious death (FC SD V.20). Forde and confessional Lutheranism differ regarding this essential issue. These differences are explained below, so that the benefits of recovering the traditional Lutheran view are apparent.

Central Theoretical Argument and Purpose

The argument commences with one primary research question, and then four subsequent questions. The overarching question to be answered is, *In what ways are Gerhard Forde's views concerning the distinction between law and gospel dissonant from what is affirmed in confessional Lutheranism?* In view of this broader consideration, the question then asked is, *What is the current state of scholarship concerning the distinction between law and gospel made within the Lutheran ecclesial tradition, including that articulated by Gerhard Forde?* The third question asked is, *What are the scriptural and*

7. Forde, *Where God Meets Man*, 15.

8. An example of the traditional Lutheran view can be found in Heinrich Schmid's *Doctrinal Theology*, 509.

9. Forde, *Where God Meets Man*, 16.

theological foundations for the distinction between law and gospel affirmed in confessional Lutheranism? Fourth, the following question is posed: *In what ways does the distinction between law and gospel articulated by Gerhard Forde compare to and contrast with the confessional Lutheran understanding?* The final research question is, *What are the implications for confessional Lutheranism of recognizing the dissonant views espoused by Gerhard Forde regarding the distinction between law and gospel?*

There are several reasons why a rejection of some of the major tenets of Forde's theology will be beneficial to the church. First, it allows for a positive function for the law in the life of the congregation. In an existential view of law and gospel, the essential *goodness* of the law is downplayed. If the law is defined by its act of killing, then there is no positive use for the law in guiding a Christian's actions in the world. However, a biblical (and historically Lutheran) theology emphasizes the essential goodness of the law in guiding God's creation. Second, it allows the exegete to be biblically faithful in expounding upon Lutheran theology. As will be demonstrated, Scripture does not refer to the law in primarily existential categories, but as a set of objective demands given by God to his creatures. When approaching the text from Forde's approach, one must distort the words of Scripture in order to remain consistent with a Radical Lutheran view of the law. Finally, the Biblical understanding of God's law will allow the Lutheran church to recapture its rich dogmatic heritage. The tenets of Radical Lutheranism are opposed to the development of Lutheran theology after the time of Luther. According to many writers, the later Lutherans were in the tradition of Melanchthon rather than that of the original Wittenberg Reformer.[10] In contradistinction to this assertion, this work argues that the richness and beauty of Lutheran theology exists not *only* in an isolated figure like Luther, but also in the dogmaticians, pastors, and exegetes who faithfully expounded upon Luther's thought in the years following his death, and especially in the Lutheran Confessions themselves.

Conclusion

Through engaging with the biblical text alongside historical and confessional documents, it becomes apparent that the novelties of Forde's exposition of law and gospel are inconsistent with the prior Lutheran tradition. Forde represents not a development of, but a departure from,

---

10. See, for example, Paulson, *Lutheran Theology*, 4.

historic Lutheranism. These differences greatly affect the proclamation of the church in the twentieth century, and thus this discussion is essential for the Lutheran church today.

The sources examined in the following chapter set a groundwork for the primary thesis of this work. When examined alongside one another, the differences between confessional Lutheran scholars and Gerhard Forde become apparent. David Scaer, Joel Biermann, Charles Arand, Scott Murray, and other Lutheran theologians explain the law-and-gospel distinction in terms of two distinct words from God, which have particular objective theological content attached. Forde, in his various writings, identifies the law and the gospel with their effects upon the listener; for him, law and gospel are synonymous with death and life.

2

Literature Review

Introduction

IN PROCEEDING WITH THE present discussion, it is imperative that a variety of contemporary writings on the subject of law and gospel be examined. In this chapter, the following question is answered: *What is the current state of scholarship concerning the distinction between law and gospel made within the Lutheran ecclesial tradition, including that articulated by Gerhard Forde?* The latter half of the twentieth century until the present time has seen a number of different important theological developments surrounding this central theme of Lutheran theology. First, some of the contemporary authors who promote a traditional confessional approach are reviewed. These writers subscribe to the Formula of Concord and emphasize consistency between their own perspectives and that of seventeenth-century Lutheran orthodoxy. The authors examined are David Scaer, Scott Murray, Joel Biermann, Charles Arand, and Jack Kilcrease. All of these writers are pastors within the Lutheran Church—Missouri Synod (with the exception of Kilcrease, who is a layperson within the Missouri Synod), and thus affirm a *quia* subscription to the Book of Concord. The utilization of these particular writings portrays that broader landscape of scholarly literature surrounding law and gospel within confessional Lutheranism, and thus prepares a groundwork for contrasts between the historic Lutheran tradition and the theological developments of Gerhard Forde.

Second, Gerhard Forde's writings on the subject of law and gospel are examined. In these works, Forde departs from the traditional understanding as promoted by the other authors. Forde has written a number of articles and books which relate to the law-gospel discussion. An examination and review of all of these materials would be impossible for this current project, and thus two particular works were chosen: *The Law-Gospel Debate* and *Where God Meets Man*. It is in these two books that Forde most clearly and extensively demonstrates his divergence from the earlier Lutheran tradition regarding the subject at hand. As this discussion proceeds, these two books in particular serve as definitional for Forde's convictions surrounding law and gospel, to be contrasted with historic confessional Lutheran theology. His other writings serve to supplement these pieces of literature throughout.

The Confessional Lutheran Landscape

All of the authors utilized in this chapter from the confessional Lutheran tradition are part of the Lutheran Church—Missouri Synod. Though there are a number of synods in America which would affirm a *quia* subscription to the Lutheran confessional documents, the Missouri Synod remains the largest, and thus contributes the most extensive amount of scholarship devoted to these issues. For the perspectives below to be most clearly understood, some background will be given regarding the Missouri Synod as well as other Lutheran church bodies in America.

While there have been Lutherans in America since the eighteenth century, they did not have a substantial presence until the mid-nineteenth century, when a number of Germans immigrated to the midwestern United States. Among the various groups that settled in the New World at that time was a small group of confessional Lutheran Saxon immigrants led by Lutheran pastor Martin Stephan to escape the rationalism and unionism of the German church. This group identified itself, in opposition to the Prussian Union, as a strictly confessional group, denying all forms of altar and pulpit fellowship with non-Lutherans. After a leadership crisis, C. F. W. Walther became the primary theologian and church leader of this group, eventually leading to the formation of the German Evangelical Lutheran Synod of Missouri, Ohio, and Other States in 1847. The name was eventually shortened and became what is known today as the Lutheran Church—Missouri Synod. This church body became a bulwark of Lutheran confessionalism in the broader Protestant American world.[1]

---

1. See Meyer, *Moving Frontiers*, which is a compilation of primary-source documents surrounding the founding of the Missouri Synod. This history is also traced in Suelflow, *Servant of the Word*.

While there were initially a number of separate groups in American Lutheranism, there were numerous efforts to unify the American Lutheran church. Broader Lutheran organizations began to develop to foster unity and ecclesiastical partnership. The earliest of these was the Evangelical Lutheran General Synod of the United States of North America. This group was rather broad in an attempt to unify various divergent streams of Lutheran thought and practice. It became identified with the so-called "American Lutheranism" of Samuel S. Schmucker, which deemphasized Lutheran distinctives and sought to redefine a number of confessional teachings.[2] The most significant of these were his rejection of the Lutheran doctrine of the real presence of Christ's body and blood in the Lord's Supper, and his subsequent revision of the Augsburg Confession.[3] Those Lutherans who believed that unity could not be achieved apart from strong doctrinal consensus formed two other groups which rejected the loose stances of the General Synod. These were the General Council and the Synodical Conference.[4]

Confessional Lutheran church bodies in the United States today derive from these two groups. First is the General Council, which split from the General Synod over its lack of confessional convictions. For some, such as the Ohio Synod, the General Council was still too moderate in its views. There were certain points of doctrine that the council declared to be "open questions," in which some variation in opinion was allowed, such as open Communion and millennialism. The Missouri Synod declined to join over these issues, as well as a difference of opinion surrounding the doctrine of election, and helped formulate the Synodical Conference. This organization included, along with the Missouri Synod, the Wisconsin Evangelical Lutheran Synod and the Evangelical Lutheran Synod.[5] Those church bodies which joined the Synodical Conference allowed for no deviation from the Lutheran Confessions and argued for strict closed Communion.

Eventually, the Synodical Conference would split apart when the Wisconsin Evangelical Lutheran Synod broke fellowship with the Lutheran

---

2. Gritsch, *History of Lutheranism*, 189–194.

3. It is worth noting that even the General Synod rejected Schmucker's attempts to adopt the modified Augsburg Confession.

4. A fourth group, the United Synod of the South, was defined primarily regionally rather than theologically, but it tended toward confessionalism.

5. Gritsch, *History of Lutheranism*, 194–199.

Church—Missouri Synod.[6] Despite the lack of fellowship between these church bodies, they both remain committed to the teachings of the Lutheran Confessions and hold to a strongly Lutheran identity in opposition to the broader world of Protestantism. Along with these two synods, the American Association of Lutheran Churches, whose predecessor bodies largely came from the General Conference, holds to a strong *quia* subscription to the Book of Concord.[7] They are also in altar and pulpit fellowship with the Lutheran Church—Missouri Synod. Though there are a number of strictly confessional pastors and theologians within all American Lutheran church bodies, the position of a strong *quia* subscription is held officially by the Lutheran Church—Missouri Synod, the Wisconsin Evangelical Lutheran Synod, the Evangelical Lutheran Synod, the American Association of Lutheran Churches, and some smaller church bodies which do not have a substantial theological or ecclesiastical presence.

As the views of confessional Lutheran writers and those of Gerhard Forde are examined, some of the differences between various Lutheran bodies in North America reflect these theological divergences. Forde was a member of the Evangelical Lutheran Church in America, which does not require a full confessional subscription from its pastors, which is why Forde himself is critical of the Formula of Concord. Forde's students, who explicate similar theological convictions, are found within the North American Lutheran Church as well as the Lutheran Churches in Mission for Christ. These bodies allow for more theological variation than those previously associated with the Synodical Conference. This is not to say that there are no critics of Forde in those church bodies either, as David Yeago (a member of the NALC), for example, has written various criticisms in response to Radical Lutheranism.[8] Conversely, there are many within the Lutheran Church—Missouri Synod who have been influenced by Forde, despite their confessional convictions.

The most influential contemporary scholarship that exists in the confessional Lutheran tradition, including those writers in the Lutheran Church—Missouri Synod, demonstrates some of these divergences between confessional orthodox Lutheranism and the writings of Gerhard Forde. This is demonstrated below as the writings from these two different traditions are explained and evaluated.

6. Zimmerman, *Seminary in Crisis*, 15.
7. This history is catalogued in Lindberg, *To Tell the Truth*.
8. Yeago, "Gnosticism."

Lex Aeterna

Writings from the Confessional Lutheran Tradition

David Scaer

The most recent book-length treatment of law and gospel from a confessional Lutheran dogmatic perspective is David P. Scaer's *Law and Gospel and the Means of Grace*. This is the eighth volume in the *Confessional Lutheran Dogmatics* series published by Luther Academy Press. This series is widely used within the Missouri Synod and other theologically conservative Lutheran synods. This text thus summarizes several of the prominent ideas surrounding law and gospel within these church bodies, and particularly within the realm of scholarly discourse among professors. In this text, Scaer presents a systematic exposition of the Lutheran distinction between law and gospel in light of Scripture, the Lutheran Confessions, and the Lutheran dogmatic tradition. Throughout, Scaer interacts with contemporary interpretations of the law-gospel dialectic, and thus defends the traditional formulation of the law-gospel distinction over against some contemporary formulations.

The terms "law" and "gospel" have been used in numerous ways throughout Christian history and in the Lutheran tradition. As Scaer notes, both the terms "law" and "gospel" can be utilized in a broad sense.[9] The term "gospel," for example, is used as a shorthand for all of the various teachings of Jesus, which includes both commands and promises. The term "law" is also sometimes utilized to describe the entire message of the Old Testament. In the confessional Lutheran tradition, however, these terms, used in their proper sense, are to be clearly distinguished. The law has reference to God's commandments, whereas the gospel refers to God's promises in Christ. In this manner, Scaer adopts the more traditional approach to law and gospel, as taught by earlier Lutheran dogmaticians. Though he does not specifically utilize the terms *"verba Dei"* or *"opera Dei,"* he discusses the distinction in *verba Dei* categories.

Scaer is careful to distinguish the law and the gospel without polarizing them. The law and the gospel serve different functions in God's relationship to sinners, but both of those functions are necessary and good. In relationship to one's *coram Deo* standing, the law condemns the sinner, and the gospel frees the sinner. The word of the gospel does not come without the prior working of God's law, and the condemnation of God's law is never an end in itself; the final word of God is always the gospel. Scaer thus

---

9. Scaer, *Law and Gospel*, 7.

balances the dissonance between law and gospel in terms of their manner of working before God, while avoiding the polarization between law and gospel which is apparent in the writings of Gerhard Forde and others following Werner Elert.

The distinction between law and gospel is not simply another locus in a theological system. Rather, the law-gospel dialectic explains how one is to approach and apply the various topics of theology. Scaer argues that this distinction should guide preaching and practice. One cannot simply explain the commandments of God with no reference to the duty of one's listeners to obey. This is the presentation of facts, and not the correct exposition of the law. Similarly, the preacher cannot simply state the facts of Jesus' life and death and assume that he has preached the gospel; the "for you" is a necessary aspect of gospel proclamation.[10] This is an area wherein Scaer *affirms* the existential reality of the law and gospel's effects when proclaimed to the sinner, and thus demonstrates continuity with Forde and other twentieth-century Lutheran theologians. Scaer does not, however, define the law and the gospel as *only* the direct address of the preacher, devoid of theological and historical content. He is quick to point out that the "for you" of the gospel necessitates a series of historical events. Similarly, the commands of the law hinge upon objective moral commandments which are eternal in nature. In this manner, Scaer balances Elert's emphasis on the law as that which kills[11] with the scholastic Lutheran definition of the law as a set of specific moral demands.[12]

Scaer places the law-gospel distinction within the context of God's relationship to man. He demonstrates that the law and gospel do not contradict one another, but *appear* to do so from man's perspective. The tension does not exist within God, but within the sinful human creature.[13] Because of the Christian's nature as *simul iustus et peccator*, both the law and the gospel speak to him in seemingly contradictory ways. This existential tension must stand, or serious theological errors result. Scaer demonstrates that there are a variety of theological traditions which try to harmonize these two words in an unhelpful and unbiblical manner. Universalists, for ex-

---

10. Ibid., 21.

11. Elert, *Structure of Lutheranism*, 35–43.

12. Schmid, *Doctrinal Theology*, 508–520.

13. One of the primary problems that arises in modern theology is that the rejection of the doctrine of divine simplicity often leads to a God who contradicts himself. In his attempt to distinguish law from gospel, Oswald Bayer argues that "God contradicts himself" (Bayer, *Theology*, 23).

ample, resolve the seeming tension by negating the condemnation of God's law altogether, whereas Reformed double-predestinarians, by denying the *gratia universalis*, place law and gospel upon the same plane.[14] Though Scaer does not specifically mention Forde in this chapter, his solution to the seeming disparity between law and gospel answers Forde's radical opposition between law and gospel in relation to God's own character.

The gospel is a superior revelation of God to the law. This does not imply that the two words are to be polarized against one another. Instead, the gospel is greater than the law, because within the gospel is included the fulfillment of the law. It is within these two aspects of Christ's work that the seeming tension between law and gospel is resolved.[15] In order for humanity's relationship to God to be restored, justice must be satisfied. The law's demands cannot remain unfulfilled. Thus, Christ must fulfill the law's demands and serve its penalty in order for the gospel to be preached and delivered. This, as will be demonstrated, is the primary difference that arises between the confessional Lutheran tradition and Radical Lutheran proponents. For Forde, the gospel must be something radically *new*, and thus cannot include the fulfillment of God's law.[16]

Both the law and the gospel reflect the nature of God. Neither is foreign to his own being. For Scaer, the law is inherent within God's own self; it is a reflection of God's own essence and moral character. He does not decide upon human regulations arbitrarily, but demonstrates his own goodness and justice through the commandments granted to his creation. It is because of God's just and moral essence that his demands must be satisfied in order for the human race to receive justification and reconciliation with their Creator.[17] In this way, the law is an objective standard, because it relates to the eternal divine nature. It is not a temporal reality only to be surpassed by an eschatological word of gospel.

Scaer is deeply committed to the confessional Lutheran teaching regarding the law's third use. Lutherans are not antinomians, as is sometimes charged. The law serves essential functions for the Christian within the life of faith. This does not only include the law's condemnatory aspects, but the law serves as a rule of life for the believer. Scaer argues that the third use of the law is not a peripheral issue, but is essential for a proper understanding

---

14. See my discussion of double predestination in Cooper, *The Great Divide*, 13–26.
15. Scaer, *Law and Gospel*, 52.
16. Forde, *Law-Gospel Debate*, 13.
17. Scaer, *Law and Gospel*, 43.

of both theology and ethics. For the Christian, the law serves in the same manner as it did in the prelapsarian state. God's commandments are received joyfully by Christians who desire to obey them in faith.[18] This sets Scaer apart from many twentieth-century Lutheran theologians, including Werner Elert, who reject the law in its didactic function.

Scaer notes that many Lutheran theologians, while not explicitly following Elert's perspective, conflate the second and third uses of the law. In this way of speaking, the third use of the law serves as a threat to the believer. Scaer argues, in contrast to this, that insofar as one is a renewed Christian, the law is a positive word. The law, in this sense, is a description of Jesus himself, and becomes descriptive of the believer as he or she is renewed into Christ's image. This Christological emphasis is a uniqueness in Scaer's thought. Older theologians do not speak extensively of the third use of the law in a Christological manner, whereas Scaer continues to insist that the law, in its third use, continues to point the believer to Christ's fulfillment of it. For Scaer, the Christological aspect of the law's third use resolves the seeming tension of law and gospel, as well as the fact that the third use is proclaimed *after* the gospel.[19] This allows Scaer to avoid some of the common criticisms of those who reject the third use, by demonstrating that a commitment to the didactic use of God's law does not replace the gospel as God's ultimate word.

Scaer presents, throughout this volume, a traditional Lutheran approach to the distinction between law and gospel. He defends the unity of God's words, as well as their differentiation existentially when spoken to sinners. Perhaps most unique about Scaer's book is his Christological focus, which is the only place where the ultimate unity of law and gospel is to be found. This sets Scaer in contrast to the majority of Radical Lutheran theologians in the twentieth and twenty-first centuries, while he is still willing to emphasize the existential nature of law and gospel as acts of God toward the sinner.

Scott Murray

In *Law, Life, and the Living God: The Third Use of the Law in Modern American Lutheranism*, Scott R. Murray gives a comprehensive history of the relationship between law and gospel with particular attention to the third use

18. Ibid., 67.
19. Ibid., 73.

of the law in the twentieth century. Murray demonstrates where he believes problems arose in the twentieth century and contends that God's law functions in a positive manner within the Christian life. This volume is important to the discussion, because it is the most extensive presentation on the third use of the law from a confessional Lutheran perspective in response to other formulations of law and gospel in the twentieth century. Though mostly a historical theological treatise, Murray's book provides concise and helpful criticisms of a variety of perspectives on law and gospel which are opposed to the traditional Lutheran formulation.

Murray gives a number of reasons why retaining the third use of the law within Lutheran theology is essential.[20] He argues that the law is a good gift to the Christian, and that this essential goodness of the law is lost or downplayed when the third use is rejected. Murray is also concerned with antinomianism in the Lutheran tradition. Because Lutherans emphasize the free nature of the gospel so extensively, it is tempting for Lutherans to neglect or even reject the importance and necessity of sanctification. This sets Murray over against the Radical Lutheran theologians, as he agrees with Scaer on the importance and validity of the third function of God's law within the life of the believer.

The distinction between law and gospel has been at the center of theological debates for centuries. Murray gives a brief overview of some of these debates within the Reformation era itself. In Luther's time, some doubted the validity of the law in Christian preaching. John Agricola argued that only the gospel should be preached in Christian congregations. The law is for the courts in the civil sphere. Luther reacted against Agricola with a series of theses on antinomianism. The Formula of Concord similarly found it necessary to explain the proper relationship between law and gospel within the Christian life. A number of theologians spoke negatively about the law in relationship to the Christian; thus, Article VI of the Formula of Concord was written in defense of the third use of the law.[21] Murray argues that this debate is no less important today than it was in the sixteenth century. Consequently, contemporary theologians must address these issues in light of current theological controversies. Murray clearly lays out his presuppositions here; he is intent on a defense of the Formula's definition

---

20. Murray, *Living God*, 15.

21. Andreas Musculus was the primary figure who argued against the third use of the law.

of the law and opposed to contemporary formulations which deviate from that definition.

Within the twentieth century, several theologians began to reject the third use of the law, following the writings of Werner Elert. Murray outlines this history through three different time periods: 1940–1960, 1961–1971, and 1977–1998. In his first section, Murray demonstrates how European theology began to influence American theologians. This theological movement, which Murray labels "Neo-Lutheranism," is exemplified by the writings of George Forell and William Lazareth. For Forell, the *lex semper accusat* principal is the very essence of the law. Lazareth follows Elert and Forell here, and argues that if there is any "third use" of the law, it is simply the second use as applied to the Christian. The law has no positive function for the life of faith. Murray views this "Neo-Lutheranism" as problematic and anti-confessional. Like Scaer, he opposes any perspective on the law which is defined *solely* by its existential function. He also, like Scaer, argues that the law continues to serve a positive function to guide the Christian within his or her life of faith. Unlike some contemporary Lutherans, he does not subsume the third use of the law under the first or second.

In his evaluation of the second time period (1961–1976), Murray points out problematic movements in two groups. First are the Valparaiso theologians, and second are the LCA and ALC theologians. The theologians from Valparaiso were highly indebted to Werner Elert, arguing on an existential basis and rejecting the third use of the law. Particularly problematic in this school of thought is what Murray calls "gospel reductionism."[22] The theologians who promoted this reductionism, such as Edward H. Schroeder, argued that the distinction between law and gospel serves as the overarching hermeneutic over Scripture. Murray argues, in contrast to this, that the law-gospel distinction is not primarily a hermeneutic; "law and gospel" is not a standard which is to be placed *over* Scripture, but law and gospel are normed *by* Scripture. Murray helpfully outlines several of the areas of dissonance between confessional Lutheranism and those who are influenced by existential philosophy. For Forde and others, the law-gospel distinction has precedence over Scripture itself, which is viewed as a fallible text. As do the seventeenth-century scholastics, Murray asserts that the law-gospel distinction arises from the reading of the infallible scriptural text.

Scott Murray writes that the views of Gerhard Forde on the third use of the law are representative of a large portion of the ALC and LCA. Forde

22. Murray, *Living God*, 103.

writes within the tradition of Erlangen, being largely influenced by J. C. K. von Hofmann. In his criticism of Hofmann, Forde argues for the centrality of eschatology within the Christian gospel. He argues that the distinction between law and gospel is founded upon the distinction between the old age and the eschaton. The law is that which is a product of the old age; it is put to an end through the cross. Because of this discontinuity between the ages, a third use of the law is impossible. Insofar as he belongs to the age to come, the Christian is free from the law.[23] This freedom is not only from the law's accusation, but from the commands themselves. Thus, the law is no longer defined as the *lex aeterna*, but as that which terrifies. The law is defined by its effect. Murray argues that Forde does not confuse law and gospel in the manner that others do by speaking of "gospel imperatives" or separating divine commands from the law. However, Forde rejects the importance of ethical discourse and redefines atonement. Like Scaer, Murray functions here within a *verba Dei* perspective regarding the law-gospel paradigm. Though he also does not use this terminology, he views the law as God's commands and the gospel as his promises. Killing and making alive are then *functions* of those words.

The final period discussed by Murray (1977–1998) is one in which the third use of the law began to have a revival in Lutheran circles. Some older theologians, such as William Lazareth and Gerhard Forde, continued to reject the third use of the law, but others had a more positive perspective. David Yeago, for example, critiques Elert's narrow perspective on law and gospel, wherein the law is placed only in an accusatory position. He rejects this perspective as gnostic and antinomian. This revival of the third use of the law had an important place within the Missouri Synod as well. Theologians such as Theodore Jungkuntz, David Scaer, and Eugene Klug have published articles in defense of the positive function of God's law within the Christian life. Murray aligns himself with these theologians, and particularly those who write within the Lutheran Church—Missouri Synod. There are no clear points of disagreement between Murray and Scaer. They both function within the framework of confessional Lutheranism, reject Radical Lutheran developments, and affirm the Christological nature of the law-gospel distinction.

Murray's volume is an essential piece of scholarship surrounding the debates over law and gospel within twentieth-century Lutheranism in America. He fairly and accurately presents the positions of existential

---

23. Ibid., 130.

Lutherans as well as those who defend a traditional confessional understanding. Murray defends a traditional approach to law and gospel, including the law's third use. For Murray, the law is not simply an accusing voice, but has objective content which is related to the nature and character of God. The gospel, similarly, is not defined by how it works, but by its content, which includes the vicarious atonement of Christ.

Joel Biermann

In his book *A Case for Character*, Joel Biermann argues for a form of virtue ethics in view of Luther's distinction between the two kinds of righteousness. This ethical system is presented in contrast to contemporary trends in the Lutheran world which neglect such discussions as misplaced in light of the distinction between law and gospel. This work, which is a modified form of Biermann's doctoral dissertation, presents an alternative perspective on the law-gospel debate by proposing that the distinction between law and gospel coexists with other theological paradigms. An evaluation of this work is essential, because the two-kinds-of-righteousness distinction aids in explaining some of the important differences between a Radical Lutheran and confessional approach to the law.

Biermann argues in the context of practical pastoral ministry. He begins his work with an illustration wherein a pastor is called to preach on Col 3:18–25.[24] This particular text consists of ethical instruction in view of the gospel. However, in some contemporary Lutheran contexts, there is no third use of God's law. Therefore, such commandments take on only a condemnatory role. The pastor is thus left to simply tell his congregation that such commandments are impossible to obey. In doing this, however, the preacher neglects the broader context in which Paul teaches such ethical commandments.

The problem, according to Biermann, is that in much of contemporary Lutheran theological discourse, the *coram mundo* aspect of Christian living is negated. The Christian life is viewed almost exclusively as a vertical reality, wherein God's law condemns the sinner, and his gospel consequently justifies the sinner. In this context, there is no place for the law's third use, since the law cannot serve this function *coram Deo*. Because this has happened, there is no consistent Lutheran framework in which ethics can be explained. This is where Biermann's proposal is essential for this study. By

---

24. Biermann, *Case for Character*, 1.

distinguishing between these two aspects of Christian existence, one is able to expound upon the positive function of God's law without encroaching upon the centrality of the gospel *coram Deo*.

There are a number of different attempts to locate the place of ethics within Lutheran theology. Biermann examines three of these and proposes a fourth.[25] First, Biermann evaluates motivation as a framework. In this view, good works are always and only a loving and free response to the grace God gives in the gospel. Biermann notes that this perspective is prominent within Lutheran academia. In this perspective, one need not focus specifically on ethical questions. Rather, one simply needs to emphasize the gospel to a greater degree. The proclamation of the gospel causes one to become more grateful, and thus good works are performed. Biermann notes, in contradistinction to this, that this approach simply does not comport with reality, or with the scriptural evidence. Texts such as Rom 7 demonstrate that the Christian's relationship to obedience is one of continual struggle, and that obedience must be intentional. Biermann also shows that Luther himself realized the need for continual admonitions of the law within the Christian life after seeing that the gospel, by itself, did not produce the extensive fruit he desired. Here, Biermann explicitly sets himself in opposition to Gerhard Forde, who emphasizes the freedom of Christian obedience as opposed to that which is constrained by law. Since the purely spontaneous approach to good works is negated, the didactic use of God's law is a necessity in the Christian life.

The second ethical proposal that Biermann evaluates is law and gospel as a framework. Some have purported that law and gospel is an all-encompassing theological framework, whereby the entire reality of the Christian life is encapsulated. The manner in which this has been utilized, in some contemporary writers, negates the third use of the law; thus law and gospel are viewed as a polarity. The opposition that law and gospel have existentially in one's *coram Deo* relationship becomes definitional of both concepts. This is the perspective of Werner Elert, Gerhard Forde, and Radical Lutheran theologians. Lutheran theologians are consequently left without any means to answer important ethical questions regarding *coram mundo* living. Biermann concludes that the distinction between law and gospel, when "used as an overall framework . . . is finally detrimental to the vitality of Lutheranism."[26] There must then be another means by which Lutheran

25. Ibid., 108–133.
26. Ibid., 118.

theology is equipped to address ethical concerns. Here is where Biermann gives his own unique contribution to the contemporary law-gospel debates.

The previous discussion leads Biermann to argue that there must be another paradigm that serves alongside a traditional law-gospel structure which allows for consistent and thoroughgoing ethical and moral instruction. He first explains the "two kinds of righteousness" framework, as first proposed by Robert Kolb and Charles Arand.[27] This framework helps to explain that law and gospel are not contradictory words of God; they simply function in two different realms. All people live *coram Deo* and *coram mundo*. Before God, the law functions in a condemnatory manner. God's commandments demonstrate one's inability to earn righteousness before the heavenly courts, and thus ultimately point one to the gospel. In this realm, it is the gospel which comes as God's final word to the sinner. Before the world, however, the gospel does not serve this same function. Instead, the human creature is pointed to God's law in its third use so that one's creaturely duties are made clear. In this framework, Elert's commitment to the gospel as God's final word is affirmed, since that is God's final word *coram Deo*. However, due to the reality of the other realm in which the Christian lives, the law has abiding validity. Though this is a helpful complementary paradigm to law and gospel, Biermann argues that there is still one primary flaw in the two-kinds-of-righteousness paradigm which he seeks to address by a fourth proposal.

Biermann argues that the two-kinds-of-righteousness framework is still inadequate in addressing Christian living. Without further distinctions between kinds of righteousness in the *coram mundo* realm, there is no place for discussing Christian ethics in particular. If horizontal righteousness is only of one kind, then there is no reason to distinguish between the unbeliever's civic righteousness and the Christian's sanctification. When explaining active righteousness, Melanchthon often speaks of civil, or philosophic, righteousness; Luther usually references the good deeds which flow from faith. These two kinds of righteousness must be distinguished for one to be consistent with both Scripture and the Lutheran confessional documents.

The answer to this dilemma, according to Biermann, is to distinguish not between just *two* kinds of righteousness, but *three* kinds of righteousness. He defines these as governing righteousness, justifying righteousness, and conforming righteousness.[28] Each of these types of righteousness cor-

27. Ibid., 118.
28. Ibid., 130.

responds to one of the three traditional uses of the law within Lutheran theology. Governing, or civil, righteousness corresponds to the first use of the law. This righteousness is one which even the unbeliever can attain through reason and moral instruction. The second type of righteousness is justifying, or passive, righteousness. This identifies one's righteous status in Christ *coram Deo*. The third is conforming righteousness, which is the righteousness that the believer performs as a result of faith. This is identical with the traditional doctrine of sanctification. In contrast to Kolb, Biermann distinguishes between the righteousness one performs in faith and that which is done by the unbeliever. This allows for a fully orbed and confessional teaching regarding the various uses of the law. While Forde conflates the first and third uses of the law, Biermann provides a structure whereby both can be affirmed in their unique spheres.

Biermann's work helpfully explains some of the problems with certain contemporary formulations of the law-gospel dialectic. By distinguishing between the three kinds of righteousness, Biermann demonstrates that the law and the gospel are not contradictory words, and the law does not always play a purely negative role within the life of the believer. The law is not purely condemnatory, but serves as a guide within the believer's existence in God's creation. By distinguishing between governing and conforming righteousness, Biermann also shows that the law does not play a role *only* in the civil sphere. Ethical instruction and positive exhortation in accord with God's commandments are an essential aspect of ecclesiastical life. This proposal serves as a further development of the traditional law-gospel framework as explained by Scaer and Murray. By distinguishing between these two spheres of human existence, the goodness and differences between law and gospel can be more thoroughly explained.

Joel Biermann and Charles Arand

In their essay "Why the Two Kinds of Righteousness?," Joel Biermann and Charles Arand introduce the distinction between the two kinds of righteousness within Lutheran thought and demonstrate its importance for the theology of the church. Throughout the article, they criticize what they view as a law-gospel reductionism within the Lutheran theological world. This article explicitly explains the distinction between the *verba Dei* and *opera Dei* which is fundamental to understanding the differences between Forde and confessional Lutheran proposals.

Literature Review

Arand and Biermann perceive several problems in the Lutheran church related to the relationship between faith and works. They assert that, due to the prominent emphasis on justification in the Lutheran tradition, some have neglected to speak about sanctification and the role of obedience in the Christian life. They desire to remedy this problem by recapturing Luther's distinction between the two kinds of righteousness as a means to explain the relationship between faith and works. The authors of this article define righteousness in relation to the "design specifications" surrounding one's relationships.[29] God created man in two essential relationships: to himself and to others. The manner in which one is righteous in each of these realms differs. Before God, righteousness is passively received; before the neighbor, it is lived and performed. The gospel rules one's *coram Deo* existence, and the law directs one's actions *coram mundo*. What is particularly important in this discussion is that Arand and Biermann focus on the *definition* of righteousness, which has sometimes been ignored within the discussion surrounding law and gospel. One's definition of righteousness will greatly influence how one understands the demands and functions of God's law. The connection between righteousness and "design specifications" gives more theological impetus to the third use of God's law.

The distinction between the two kinds of righteousness is intimately related to one's understanding of law and gospel. Arand and Biermann note that the concept of law and gospel has been understood in two different senses. First, it refers to the *verba Dei* (words, or grammar, of God); second, it refers to the *opera Dei* (actions of God).[30] In the Lutheran tradition, the phrase "law and gospel" often has reference to the effects of both words of God upon the hearer. The law kills, and the gospel makes alive. When this is all that is said about the law and the gospel, problems arise. One might begin to speak as if *the law itself* is a problem, rather than the sinner who is condemned by it. Though not likely the intention, Forde and other Radical Lutheran proponents use language that makes it sound as if this is the case. This is why, according to Arand and Biermann, in their most proper sense, the law and the gospel refer simply to the two manners in which God speaks: by command and by promise. It is these definitions of law and gospel which differentiate this approach from many twentieth-century writers.

For a large portion of Lutheran history, antinomianism has been viewed as the ultimate enemy, and thus the *opera Dei* gained precedence

---

29. Arand and Biermann, "Why the Two Kinds," 118.
30. Ibid., 123.

over the *verba Dei*. This was a necessary emphasis in the Reformation era and in the time of Pietism. In contemporary theological discourse, however, the opposite problem has arisen. Arand and Biermann are concerned that another form of "one kind of righteousness" has arisen which ignores the importance of sanctified living. When this occurs, the law is placed in a solely accusatory position, and Melanchthon's statement *lex semper accusat* becomes *lex sole accusat*. The law and the gospel are viewed as polarizing concepts, and the goodness of God's law is downplayed. Arand and Biermann's emphasis on the *verba Dei*, along with their focus on *coram mundo* existence, allows one to avoid several of the problems that arise in contemporary Lutheran sources.

For Arand and Biermann, contemporary Lutheranism finds itself in a unique dilemma, wherein the law-and-gospel distinction is understood in an antinomian manner. They argue, in contrast to some contemporary writers, that Lutherans must recapture the two-kinds-of-righteousness distinction as a means by which the goodness of God's law can be explained, especially with reference to life in this world. By distinguishing between the *verba Dei* and the *opera Dei*, Arand and Biermann make explicit something which is implicit in other confessional Lutheran treatments of the law-gospel distinction. This distinction is essential to expound upon the further differences which exist between Lutheran confessionalism and Forde's Radical Lutheranism.

Charles Arand

The distinction between the two kinds of righteousness is at the heart of the Lutheran Confessions. This is Charles Arand's contention in "Two Kinds of Righteousness as a Framework for Law and Gospel in the Apology." Throughout this essay, Arand argues that law and gospel, in and of itself, is not an adequate framework whereby one can interpret all theological claims. Instead, Arand asserts, one must look to the distinction between passive and active righteousness. The importance of this writing, for confessional Lutheranism, is that Arand attempts to demonstrate that the two-kinds-of-righteousness distinction is not a new development, but arises within the confessions themselves, and also serves as a framework for explaining the distinction between law and gospel.

Arand argues that law and gospel cannot be viewed as the interpretive grid for the Apology of the Augsburg Confession, particularly because of articles XXII–XXVIII. Melanchthon, in these articles, expounds upon practical aspects of Christian living, which are not explained by the use of a strict law-gospel dichotomy. Arand concludes that the two-kinds-of-righteousness model is a more comprehensive distinction to understand Melanchthon's discussion of both theology and practice. Melanchthon does not place the law in a solely accusatory position *coram Deo* in his Apology, but defends the goodness of the law as a guide for Christian living. If Melanchthon himself utilizes such a distinction, then it is demonstrated that the Lutheran tradition from its very beginning has had a different conception of law and gospel than the proponents of Radical Lutheranism.

Melanchthon writes extensively about active righteousness in the Apology. He speaks about civic righteousness, philosophic righteousness, and the righteousness of works. Arand argues that these are all synonyms for active righteousness. Unlike Biermann, Arand does not distinguish between the active righteousness of the unregenerate person and Christian sanctification, though such a distinction is clear within the Apology itself. Along with active righteousness, Arand demonstrates that Melanchthon has several phrases which refer to passive righteousness, including "Christian righteousness," "the righteousness of God," and "the righteousness of the heart." The two kinds of righteousness, passive and active, according to Arand, correspond to the two aspects of human life: life before God, and life before other human creatures. The law and the gospel are to be divided in light of these two types of relationships. The vertical relationship with God is determined by the gospel, and the horizontal relationship with others is guided by the law. Arand does not seek to reject the traditional Lutheran contention regarding the primacy of the law's second use. The law always accuses *coram Deo*. However, the law is essentially good, and thus gives one guidance according to its third use. This allows for one to contend that the gospel *is* God's final word regarding the Creator-creature relationship, but it is *not* the final word in the creature-creature relationship.

While the distinction between law and gospel and that between the two kinds of righteousness are not identical, Arand argues that one cannot properly understand one without the other. Without the two-kinds-of-righteousness distinction, the law is placed in a solely accusatory position, and one is left without any concrete framework whereby ethical questions can be discussed. Arand's article demonstrates that the two-kinds-of-righteousness distinction is a helpful means to clarify the confessional teaching surrounding law and gospel. As the confessional teaching is examined in the following chapter, Arand's work remains an essential piece of literature in understanding the context of law and gospel within the writings of the Lutheran Reformers.

Jack Kilcrease

Professor of theology at Aquinas College and lay theologian Jack Kilcrease wrote a doctoral dissertation and two subsequent articles on the theology of Gerhard Forde from a confessional Lutheran approach. His dissertation, titled *The Self-Donation of God: Gerhard Forde and the Question of Atonement in the Lutheran Tradition*, is both an exposition and critique of Forde's thought in light of traditional Lutheran theology. Following his thesis, Kilcrease wrote two essays expositing these same themes for *Concordia Theological Quarterly*. The first is "Gerhard Forde's Doctrine of the Law: A Confessional Lutheran Critique," and the second is titled, "Gerhard Forde's Theology of Atonement and Justification: A Confessional Lutheran Response." In each of these works, Kilcrease affirms many of the positions of Forde, while also echoing many of the critiques of his approach to the law and atonement as found in Murray, Biermann, Scaer, and other Lutheran critics. The two primary areas of critique that Kilcrease offers are law and atonement. Each of these is explained here.

In his criticism of Forde's perspective on the law, Kilcrease draws primarily on the definition of law in the Formula of Concord and on Luther's own writings. While Forde defines the law chiefly in terms of an existential dread which leads one to the gospel, the Formula of Concord defines the law as an eternal and unchangeable standard. Here, Kilcrease affirms Murray's criticisms of Forde as inconsistent with the historic Lutheran tradition. Unlike some other critics, however, Kilcrease does not propose that Forde's definition of the law should be rejected. Instead, he argues that an existential view of the law and the perspective that the law represents God's eternal will should and must be held together. While Kilcrease certainly does not reject the third use of the law, he speaks of the law in primarily a negative sense. With Forde, he agrees that the law always accuses, and can even in a sense be defined as that which accuses. This does not, however, temporalize the law. Instead, God's eternal will is to punish sin, and thus, the law is both eternal and condemnatory. In contrast to this, Forde purports that the law cannot be eternal, since it only exists in the present evil age and will cease to exist eschatologically. Kilcrease is largely in agreement with the previous authors examined, though he is somewhat more sympathetic to Forde's approach by emphasizing its negative existential condemnatory nature.

Kilcrease draws upon a distinction made by Theodosius Harnack between the essence and office of the law. This is similar to the distinction made by Biermann and Arand between the law as the *verba Dei* and the *opera Dei*. While the essence of the law, as God's eternal will, remains the same, the office of the law differs before and after the fall, as well as in the present and eschatological ages. Forde rejects this distinction by defining the essence of the law by its condemning office. As Kilcrease notes, this would, if consistently applied, negate the objectivity of the law altogether. The law itself must precede sin, if sin is to be defined as a violation of God's will. While Forde does not purely make the law a subjective reality, this seems to be the consistent application of his perspective. Kilcrease also notes that Forde's approach seems to negate the concrete proclamation of specific law to convict sinners. It is more appropriate, instead, to hold both Forde's emphasis on the condemnatory existential nature of the law and the eternal nature of God's commands together. As Kilcrease argues, Luther is able to speak in both ways.

As a Missouri Synod Lutheran holding to a *quia* subscription to the Book of Concord, Kilcrease affirms the third use of God's law in contrast to Forde. He argues, however, that Forde does not really deny the third use practically, though he does not utilize that language. Rather than rejecting the third use altogether, Forde conflates the civil and didactic functions of the law, purporting that the civil use of the law is sufficient to guide the Christian. In fact, when Forde criticizes the third use of the law, he does so with a faulty understanding of what the third use actually is. *Coram Deo*, according to Kilcrease, the law is silenced by the gospel as the final word to the sinner. However, the law continues to demonstrate God's will to the human creature. It does this primarily in a negative sense, as the law continues to subdue and suppress the old sinful nature of the Christian. Utilizing language that Forde cites to critique the third function of the law, Kilcrease writes that the third use "cannot rightly be characterized as a pleasant or non-threatening form of the law."[31] While Scaer, Biermann, and Arand all speak of the third use of the law in a primarily positive manner, as positive guidelines for the Christian to follow, Kilcrease speaks in a largely negative manner.[32]

---

31. Kilcrease, "Doctrine of the Law," 172.

32. This difference is especially apparent in Scaer's connection between the law in its prelapsarian function and the third use.

The divergence which exists between Kilcrease and some other confessional Lutherans is apparent in his review of Joel Biermann's *A Case for Character* published in *Logia: A Journal of Lutheran Theology*. In this review, Kilcrease argues that the situation Biermann paints of a Lutheranism that does not preach positively on ethical matters does not actually exist. He is particularly critical of Biermann's utilization of virtue ethics as a manner to speak about the Christian's active righteousness in the world. While Biermann argues that Luther only rejected the ideas of habituation and virtue in the context of justification, Kilcrease purports that the Reformer rejected these concepts altogether. To adopt a framework of virtue ethics is to argue that God gives man some kind of potentiality which he can then use in a process of self-creation or self-actualization. In this context, Kilcrease is also critical of the two-kinds-of-righteousness framework. While he does not reject such a distinction altogether, Kilcrease argues that the contemporary utilization of such a framework is deficient. He purports that contemporary authors, such as Biermann, have mistakenly utilized the distinction between these two righteousnesses as an overall framework which displaces the law-gospel distinction from its central position. In his view, Biermann has "little appreciation for the sanctifying reality of the gospel."[33] His theology is ethically driven and ignores the effectual nature of God's word and sacraments to change the sinner.

Forde's rejection of the eternal and immutable nature of the divine law leads to an understanding of the atonement which differs from traditional Lutheranism. Kilcrease is critical of his position on this issue and proposes a correction to Forde's view on this subject. For Forde, any satisfaction idea of the atonement is to be rejected for two primary reasons. First, the idea that Jesus must actively obey or passively satisfy specific commandments ultimately misses the eschatological newness of the gospel. For Forde, the atonement is the bringing about of a new age rather than Christ fulfilling the law, which belongs to the old age. Second, this ultimately subsumes the gospel under the law, because the gospel itself is defined by obedience to the law, even if it is in a substitutionary sense. As a confessional Lutheran, Kilcrease rejects Forde's proposal as inadequate and inconsistent with the Lutheran Confessions.

While Kilcrease appreciates the connection that Forde makes between justification and atonement, as well as his rejection of various liberal and feminist atonement theories, he argues that Forde's perspective is essentially

---

33. Kilcrease, *"Case for Character,"* 89.

Kantian. Forde functions, consciously or not, from a great noumenal/phenomenal divide. The Radical Lutheran theologian approaches the law not in the sense of the thing-in-itself, but in terms of the effect it has upon the one hearing its proclamation. The idea of a *lex aeterna* that Christ must vicariously fulfill is too abstract and inaccessible for Forde. While Kilcrease affirms, in some sense, the connection between the hidden God and the law (at least in terms of its office), he does not relegate the law to some hidden sphere of knowledge, but approaches it through the concrete commands of God as explicitly stated in Scripture. This criticism of Forde as essentially Kantian in his approach to the law appears to be a unique observation of Kilcrease.

The essential problem, in Kilcrease's view of Forde's doctrine of atonement, is the manner in which he explains the doctrine of justification. While Forde correctly explains the necessary connection between one's view of atonement and justification, this also means that his own faulty understanding of atonement leads to a faulty approach to justification. While traditional Lutheranism argues for justification *extra nos* through the alien righteousness of Christ, Forde locates justification within the Christian. According to the Lutheran scholastics, justification is a forensic and external ruling; for Forde, justification is an act wherein the believer is brought from death to life. The second problem with Forde's doctrine of justification, according to Kilcrease, is its negation of the goodness of creation. Forde works with a strong old age–new age distinction. While this distinction on its own is biblical, he speaks of these two ideas as an absolute dichotomy. The manner in which Forde speaks of new creation sounds as if the old is replaced by the new, rather than actually renewed. In this way, Forde approaches the Flacian heresy in identifying the created human creature with sin and the regenerate Christian as a totally new subject.[34] According to Kilcrease, there must be *some* continuity between the old and new creation in order for redemption to be a reality.

Throughout his writings on Forde, Kilcrease brings a number of beneficial and unique insights into these discussions on law, gospel, and atonement. Where his writings are most unique are in his criticisms of Forde's view of atonement. While Murray touches on these issues, Kilcrease deals in a more in-depth manner on the subject. What is especially insightful is

---

34. Matthias Flacius was a sixteenth-century Reformer who argued that sin is not accidental to the human creature, but constitutes one's very essence. This is rejected in Article I of the Formula of Concord.

his evaluation of Forde's two-age contrast in light of the article of creation. In other areas, however, his criticisms of Forde are less than adequate. While distancing himself from Forde in a number of ways, Kilcrease does not significantly depart from Forde's perspective on the Christian life. Like Forde, Kilcrease views the Christian life as a process of getting used to the fact that one is wholly justified by faith. He approaches the third use of the law in almost exclusively negative terms, and is highly critical of Biermann and others who emphasize the necessity of virtuous living with a view to a positive function of the divine commands.

Confessional Lutheran Writings: Conclusion

There are several areas of agreement and similarity between the various confessional Lutheran treatments of God's law as cited above, as well as some unique contributions to the debate in each text. Each work speaks about the law not as a purely existential reality, but as the eternal will of God as expressed in the commandments. These commands serve three distinct purposes: to guide civil righteousness, to demonstrate one's sin, and to serve as a guide for Christian living. The third use of the law is affirmed in a positive sense in each author, though Kilcrease emphasizes its negative aspects. These writers also do not speak of the law and the gospel as contradictory words, but as two distinct doctrines which affect their hearers in divergent ways. Finally, these theologians affirm the historic Lutheran doctrine of vicarious satisfaction, wherein Christ fulfills the divine law on behalf of sinful humanity through his active and passive obedience.

Though in theological agreement with one another regarding these essential points, each writer above brings his own distinctive emphasis and concerns into the theological conversation. Scaer's work is particularly beneficial in bringing the existential and theological aspects of the law-gospel distinction together. While critical of purely existential Lutheranism, Scaer appropriately defends the notion that these two doctrines are not merely propositional realities. That does not negate the fact that they do, however, have important precise theological content, including the active and passive obedience of Christ. Murray shows many of the important historical factors involved in the development of gospel reductionism as well as a denial of the third use of the law in the twentieth century. These historical factors enable the reader to trace the roots of some of the various beliefs promoted in contemporary theologians. Charles Arand and Joel Biermann formulate an approach to the third use of the law which helps to explain its connection to the active righteousness of the Christian. They do this by arguing for the usefulness of a "two kinds of righteousness" framework. Arand further demonstrates that this framework is found within the Lutheran Confessions and is thus not a new development. Biermann helpfully connects the first and third uses of the law with two distinct kinds of active righteousness related to the unbeliever and the believer respectively. Kilcrease demonstrates that Forde's perspective on law and atonement negates the goodness of creation and the reality of redemption rather than replacement. All of these various developments help to differentiate the confessional tradition from that of Gerhard Forde.

Gerhard O. Forde

The Law-Gospel Debate

In his first published work, Gerhard Forde examines the debates surrounding law and gospel from the nineteenth through mid-twentieth centuries. He traces the academic treatments of this subject within Lutheran theology from J. C. K. von Hofmann through the writings of Karl Barth and his opponents. Throughout the work, Forde seeks to demonstrate that Lutheran orthodoxy functioned with an improper view of the law, which led to a number of theological problems. Hofmann and other Lutherans rightly argue against the scholastic understanding, but according to Forde, they still have not captured the unique eschatological nature of the Christian gospel. This book is a reworked version of Forde's doctoral dissertation. It is his clearest presentation of his perspective on the distinction between law and gospel. The ideas developed in this book are foundational for all of his later writings on the topic. In it he discusses his disagreements with the scholastic Lutheran tradition in a clear and concise manner, and it is thus the most important work in distinguishing Forde's perspective from that of traditional Lutheranism.

Forde frames this book around the Lutheran orthodox understanding of the law and its subsequent rejection by later Lutheran scholars. Forde argues that scholasticism operated with a "static-ontological concept of divine law."[35] For the seventeenth-century theologians, the law is an eternal and unchanging standard. This standard is a reflection of God's own nature

---

35. Forde, *Law-Gospel Debate*, 4.

and character. This is the perspective echoed by all of the previous writers examined thus far. Forde purports that this conviction is at the heart of the entire orthodox system. Without it, theology must be radically revised. In this sense, orthodox writers would agree. Murray, for example, demonstrates throughout his work how the difference in one's understanding of the law radically affects the entirety of one's theological system. This has a number of theological implications which Forde views to be problematic. First, this concept of *lex aeterna* limits the freedom of God. Rather than offering forgiveness freely, God is under compulsion to act according to a law that exists within himself. This leads to the second problem of the atonement. For orthodoxy, the atonement has to fit within a judicial scheme. God's justice must be satisfied in order for him to grant justification, and therefore Christ's life and death are viewed as necessary for God to be able to forgive. This, according to Forde, negates any understanding of real mercy and forgiveness. Here, Forde demonstrates a differentiation with Scaer, who argues that the ultimate unity of law and gospel is to be found in Christ, and particularly through his atoning death. This leaves Forde unable to propose that there is any real unity or reconciliation between law and gospel. Third, this concept of an eternal law resulted in both the law and the gospel being defined by specific doctrinal content. In Forde's mind, this makes the gospel itself into a new kind of law. At the heart of this is the traditional understanding of the atonement as *satisfactio vicaria*, as defended by Scaer and Murray. Following Francis Pieper's *Christian Dogmatics*, LCMS theologians place a high emphasis on Christ's work of substitution. Fourth, this static understanding of God and his law contributes to a static understanding of revelation, which resulted in the formulation of biblical inerrancy. The final problem, in Forde's view, is that the scholastics speak then not simply of the law in its killing function, but argue that there is a third use, wherein the law serves as a guide for Christian living. Thus, Forde's proposal is opposed to the "two kinds of righteousness" paradigm as explained by Biermann and Arand.

The shift from the Lutheran orthodox conception of divine law begins with the Erlangen theologian J. C. K. von Hofmann. Hofmann sought to approach theology in a different manner than the seventeenth-century Lutherans, rejecting biblical infallibility. He did this by extrapolating a theological system from a personal experience of salvation. This experience is not an individualistic one as it was in some pietistic systems, but the Christian experience as mediated by the church community. Hofmann then extrapolates the history of salvation from the personal experience of salvation. Thus, one begins with personal experience, and then reasons to historical reality, which gives a basis to this experience. Lutheran orthodox theologians begin with the starting point of an infallible Scripture. From this starting point, the role of the theologian is to repeat and explain the teachings of Scripture. For Hofmann, experience replaces Scripture as such a starting point.[36] This explains some of the reasons for disagreement among confessional Lutheran and other Lutheran theologians. One's theological starting point has profound implications for the doctrinal propositions one makes.

Hofmann was dedicated, essentially, to a *Heilsgeschichte* methodology. Christian doctrine must not be exposited in an abstract otherworldly sphere, but explained through the means of history. In this way, Hofmann reflects some prominent themes of German idealism. Forde notes that it is Schelling, in particular, who influences Hofmann's system.[37] Within this understanding, Hofmann emphasizes the atonement not as a payment in a legal soteriological scheme, but as that which creates a new humanity. In the incarnation, God's loving will and divine wrath meet, creating a synthesis (in Hegelian terms) wherein righteousness is realized on behalf of the human race. Hofmann thus undercuts the basis of the entire Lutheran orthodox system in rejecting a legal approach to the atonement. Thus, law and gospel are no longer reconcilable in the same manner that confessional writers argue.

Within the *Heilsgeschichte* scheme of Hofmann, law takes on a new purpose and meaning. It is no longer the *lex aeterna* through which God's nature is understood; rather, the law is simply one part of redemptive history which has been surpassed. Hofmann views the law as that which was uniquely given to Israel, and which thus has no eternal character. In this way, he does not speak of atonement in traditional scholastic terms, nor is he bound to speak of a third use of the divine law. Though Forde ultimately rejects the *Heilsgeschichte* methodology of Hofmann, he argues that Hofmann has rightly understood the problems inherent within Protestant scholasticism, and is highly indebted to Hofmann's contention that the law is not eternal in nature. Forde is highly influenced by Hofmann's theology,

---

36. This is not experience in a pure subjectivist sense, as the modern reader might assume. This experience occurs through the Christian community, with a special emphasis on the sacraments.

37. Forde, *Law-Gospel Debate*, 25.

and in particular his arguments against Lutheran scholasticism. This lays the groundwork for Forde's disagreement with older Lutheran theological systems.

In the second section of his work, Forde examines the thought of two figures after Hofmann whose work on Luther's theology has been influential in the twentieth century: Theodosius Harnack and Albrecht Ritschl. Harnack, like the old Lutheran orthodox dogmaticians, held to an idea of vicarious atonement. While Forde disagrees with Harnack on this point, he argues that Harnack brought some important themes within Luther's thought to light. The most important of these is the dialectical nature of Luther's theology. He does this by speaking of God in two particular ways: "in Christ" and "outside of Christ."[38] This is not a statement about natural theology versus revealed theology, as might be the case in the seventeenth-century system. Rather, God outside of Christ is identified with law and wrath, whereas God in Christ is identified with love and the gospel. This "in Christ" and "outside of Christ" distinction is influential within Forde's thought. He uses Harnack's development to write, in later works, about the distinction between "God preached" and "God not preached," which echoes Harnack's thought. Through this framework, Forde also identifies God "outside of Christ" with law, and God "in Christ" with the gospel.

Ultimately, Forde rejects these various attempts to explicate the law-gospel distinction in the nineteenth century. While they rightly reject the scholastic system, these writers have still failed to capture the eschatological newness of the gospel. This is largely done by the exclusion of the law from one's theological system. While orthodoxy failed in placing the law within its theological system as an underlying structure, nineteenth-century theology made the equally problematic error of rejecting law altogether. Forde argues that as much as these theologians were right to critique Protestant scholasticism, they failed to understand the eschatological nature of the Christian message. According to Forde, this eschatological element was not recognized until the twentieth century. It is this eschatological commitment which is foundational for Forde's entire theological system and demonstrates where the differences between him and other theologians remain.

Forde approaches the contemporary law-gospel debate from the perspective of Karl Barth's theology. In contrast to traditional Lutheran theology, Barth argues that both the law and the gospel are words of grace. It is in fact an act of grace that God speaks to man at all. This is due to the Barthian

38. Ibid., 84.

dialectic, which is not between law and gospel, but the word of God and the word of man. As words of God, there is an inherent unity in law and gospel. God's word is always a word of grace, and the law comes as another form of the gospel. Thus, the order for Barth is not law-gospel, but instead gospel-law. Barth's rejection of the traditional Lutheran view on this issue is the foundation upon which much of the discussion surrounding law and gospel has begun in the last century.

At first glance, it may appear that Barth rejects the traditional "second use" of the law altogether. However, Barth does confess that the law, in some sense, condemns sinners. This is not, however, God's intended *purpose* of the law. Instead, this is the result of a human *misuse* of the law. In this human misuse, the law becomes a revelation of God's wrath and thus kills the sinner. This misuse of the law is not only an occasional occurrence, but it seems to be an absolute necessity for one to come to faith.[39] In this way, Barth confesses some type of traditional law-gospel dichotomy, even though he would prefer not to utilize traditional Lutheran terminology. Yet, following the gospel, the law is then proclaimed. Forde argues that Barth is not speaking of a traditional "third use" of God's commands. Rather than speaking of the *lex aeterna*, Barth explains the law as a word of address to man in his concrete and individual situation. It is, in some sense, an eschatological word. It is specifically this eschatological nature of God's word which Forde identifies as beneficial within this ongoing dialogue. This move in Barthian theology, as well as Barth's emphasis on God's word as one of address, is something which extends throughout the writings of Forde and stands at the center of his continual critique of Lutheran orthodoxy.

There were a number of responses to Barth in the twentieth century from a variety of Lutheran theologians. Forde discusses the response of five of these writers: Elert, Thielicke, Wingren, Iwand, and Ebeling. Though not all identical, these responses share some common themes which are influential upon Forde's thought. In contrast to Barth, all of these writers argue that the law is to be identified with God's wrath, and by its nature, it condemns. This is not a human "misuse" of the law, but is part of the law itself. Forde defines Thielicke's view, writing, "Law and gospel must be kept separate even if this gives the appearance of a dualism, because this conceptual form is necessary to preserve the nature of God as wrath and love."[40] In the scholastic writers, and in modern theologians such as Scaer and

---

39. Forde, *Law-Gospel Debate*, 142.
40. Ibid., 154.

Murray, an ultimate unity was sought between law and gospel, wherein Jesus fulfilled the law in order to satisfy the demands of God's justice. In these twentieth-century writers, no such synthesis is attempted. They simply let the paradox of wrath and grace stand. Here, there appears to be disunity within God's own being, which identifies a key problem in Forde's system. This also results in a rejection of the "third use" of God's law, especially in the writings of Elert. There is no distinction between *coram Deo* and *coram mundo* realities of life.

Forde sees the solution to this debate in recapturing Luther's own theology, which he views as inconsistent with Lutheran orthodoxy. Citing Lauri Haikola, Forde notes that the primary difference between Luther and later orthodoxy is in their respective definitions of God's law. For orthodoxy, the law is eternal in nature and character, and God must satisfy its demands in order to be truly just. For Luther, the word "law" is simply the mode by which God confronts man in particular situations.[41] The law is thus defined not by what it *is*, but by what it *does*. Forde rejects any attempt to separate the essence of the law from the office of the law. He thus does not distinguish between the *verba Dei* and the *opera Dei* as Arand and Biermann do. This means that the law, for Forde, is not necessarily even identified with commandments as such. Instead, the law is whatever accuses the conscience.

The difference Forde sees between his perspective and that of orthodoxy is not simply over the issue of the law. It includes differences surrounding the gospel as well. This relates, primarily, to the eschatological nature of the gospel in relation to God's law. Forde purports that the law is not in a continuous line with the gospel. The law does not need to be satisfied by Christ. This is an attempt to place old wine into new wineskins by putting the law into the content of the gospel. Instead, there is a radical discontinuity between these two words of God. The law belongs only to the old age, and the gospel to the new. The gospel is an end of the law in the full sense of that phrase. It is not its fulfillment, but simply stops the law's accusing voice. This does not mean that the law ends its purpose within the life of the believer. The Christian exists simultaneously in the old and new age. Thus, he needs the law insofar as he exists in the flesh. There is *not*, however, a third use of God's law. This would imply that the law somehow arrives *after* the gospel, thus denying its temporal nature. The law and the gospel are not identified, then, as two words of God—namely, commands

41. Ibid., 177.

and promises—but as two ages in which the Christian exists. Here, Forde disagrees with earlier Lutheran thought. Because the gospel is God's final eschatological word, no further word of God is possible.

The Law-Gospel Debate is the most extensive treatment of this theological distinction between God's two words from Gerhard Forde's theological career. Though his earliest work, the themes explored in this text extend throughout his writings. Since the majority of Forde's other books are written on a more popular level, this academic work is a necessary piece of writing in order for the reader to understand the greater theological influences and presuppositions of his other writings. He clearly demonstrates several key differences between his view on this subject and that of many previous authors, including the nature of the law, the atonement, and Christian ethics.

Where God Meets Man

In his popular book *Where God Meets Man: Luther's Down-to-Earth Approach to the Gospel*, Gerhard Forde attempts to unpack the ideas initially expounded in his dissertation to a lay audience. Throughout this volume, Forde seeks to explain a "down-to-earth" approach to the Christian gospel, and in doing so he discusses law and gospel, the atonement, the third use of the law, and many other themes pertinent to our study. This is another early work of Forde, but it expounds upon law and gospel more clearly than many of his later writings.

Forde's thesis centers around what he calls "ladder theology."[42] He argues that people naturally view the law as a ladder which leads to heaven by obedience. In its most crass form, this is a type of Pelagianism, wherein one believes that one must climb a ladder to God through moral exercise. Others, in the medieval world, viewed mystical ascent as the means by which one climbs Jacob's ladder with the ultimate goal of union with God. Though the Reformation argued against these theological movements, Forde argues that the Protestant tradition adopted its own form of ladder theology. Rather than arguing that humans must climb the ladder themselves, they simply replace the human subject with Christ. Thus, God is still reached by means of a ladder, but Christ is the one who climbs that ladder as a substitute. Forde disagrees with the Lutheran scholastic approach, as well as that of contemporary confessional Lutheran theologians.

42. Forde, *Where God*, 9.

Forde fears that in the orthodox schema, the gospel is simply made into another law. It is defined not as a new eschatological reality, but as the fulfillment of the law. He argues that the gospel is not framed by means of the law, but is an entirely new word of God. The gospel puts an end to the law. Here, the influence of Barth's emphasis on the word of God and eschatology is apparent. In this context, Forde rejects traditional views of the active and passive obedience of Christ. Christ does not need to actively obey the law on behalf of anyone, because this implies that the law results in salvation. Similarly, there is no need for Christ to pay any legal debt owed to God on the cross. Forde argues that God is not one who can be bought off, even if by the second person of the Holy Trinity. The *satisfactio vicaria* as defended by Scaer above is rejected as inconsistent with God's eschatological word of the gospel.

Following Elert, Forde argues that the law is not a specific set of demands. It is instead defined by what it does. He purports that the law is simply whatever accuses, to the point of arguing that *anything* which performs this function is "law." Rather than a ladder, Forde argues that the law is a circle around man's existence. In offers him absolutely no way out. The gospel then breaks into that circle as something entirely new, which frees him from condemnation and accusation. Like the law, the gospel is defined by its effect.[43] The gospel is that which puts an end to the voice of the law. Here, the confusion between the *opera Dei* and *verba Dei* in Forde's thought is apparent. Whatever does the divine *opera* of killing is by definition law.

Along with his redefinition of God's law, Forde expounds upon the nature of the Christian life. He rejects two central and consistent topics in Lutheran orthodoxy: progressive sanctification and the third use of the law. Regarding sanctification, Forde purports that there is no progress, but a daily resurrection. This is consistent with Forde's contention that the Christian lives between the two ages of law and gospel. To argue that one progresses in the Christian life is to, once again, buy into the ladder scheme. Even if the ladder does not *save* in this context, one is still living in an attempt to gain some sort of original righteousness. Regarding the law's third use, to argue that the law has any function following the proclamation of the gospel is to negate the law's connection to the old age, and once again, to affirm the ladder scheme. Forde's perspective, then, is exactly that which Murray demonstrates as inconsistent with the Lutheran confessional tradition.

---

43. Forde, *Where God*, 16.

Forde writes not just for the academy, but with the proclamation of the church in view. This means that his writings have profound implications for the lives of average Christians, especially in relation to what they hear from the pulpit on Sunday morning. This work demonstrates the implications of Forde's redefinition of law and gospel for the Christian life and preaching. These ideas are also apparent throughout Forde's career in his various essays and books.

Gerhard Forde's Writings: Conclusion

These two works of Gerhard Forde present only a small portion of his published volumes that address his views on law and gospel. These books are, however, the clearest and most extensive treatment of these topics, which do affect his theology in other areas as well. In these volumes, the central aspects of Forde's theology in relation to law and gospel are clear. He connects the law not with the eternal will of God, but with God's act of killing, which impacts the human creature existentially. The gospel, similarly, is defined by its effect of making alive, rather than the content inherent within it. There is, according to Forde, no need for Christ's vicarious law-keeping or death. For this to be part of the gospel is to deny the eschatological newness of the gospel. The primary theme, then, soteriologically speaking, is death and life. These existential acts constitute the heart of Christian theology and eschatology. Because of his redefinition of the law and his rejection of the supposed "static-ontological concept" of God's commandments, Forde rejects the teaching of the third use of the law and progressive sanctification in its historic sense. All of these factors lead to a radically different approach to the Christian faith and life than is found in confessional writers.

Conclusion

Within the various pieces of literature surrounding the topic of law and gospel within the past century, there are essentially two different perspectives defended by disparate theologians. First, there are those who desire to remain within the Protestant scholastic tradition. These writers, including Scaer, Biermann, Arand, and Murray, argue that the law is in its essence eternal. Though there is an existential element to the law's effect upon the human creature, its definition is rooted in God's own nature and character, rather than the human experience of divine wrath. Along with their affirmation of the *lex aeterna*, these writers view the law as an essential aspect of atonement. Because the law is part of God's own moral nature, it must be fulfilled in order for redemption to be accomplished. Thus the atonement is deeply rooted in legal metaphors. Jesus must obey God's law on behalf of the human race, and he also must pay the penalty owed by those who have broken it. For these writers, the law is not meant *only* to be obeyed by Christ, however, but the believer is called unto obedience, as feeble as that obedience might be. There is, then, a "third use" of God's law, whereby the Christian is guided in ethical decisions by divine commandments.

Second, there are those writers who follow after Hofmann in rejecting the *lex aeterna* and opt for other models of law, atonement, and obedience. Rather than God's eternal demands for his creation, law is defined as an aspect of God's wrath toward his sinful creation. Forde rejects any distinction between the law's office and the law's essence, purporting that the killing function of the law is the very *essence* of the law. This leads to a variety of other atonement models which reject the penal substitution theory proposed by Lutheran orthodoxy. For Forde, Christ's death is just that: a death. There is essentially no meaning *behind* the cross, but simply the event of the cross itself. Because the law's office is its killing function alone, there is then no place for a third use of the law. Instead, ethical decisions are to be made in each particular situation according to what challenges are faced at that moment. Laws change, and are thus not eternal.

In this chapter, the question, *What is the current state of scholarship concerning the distinction between law and gospel made within the Lutheran ecclesial tradition, including that articulated by Gerhard Forde?* has been answered as these writings have been evaluated. There is a divide between confessional Lutheran scholarship surrounding law and gospel and the writings of Gerhard Forde. Whereas the traditional Lutheran approach defines law and gospel first in terms of their content, and secondly in terms of their impact upon the sinner, Forde writes about them as almost exclusively existential realities. Law and gospel are defined not by what they *are*, but by what they *do*. This affects one's views on the third use of the law, the atonement, and sanctification. As these differences become apparent, the theological and biblical foundations for the traditional confessional teaching are examined in light of these contemporary challenges. This is the subject addressed in the following chapter. Following this exposition, these two disparate teachings are compared to one another in relation to their respective implications for theology and life.

3

The Scriptural and Theological Foundations for the Distinction between Law and Gospel in Confessional Lutheranism

Introduction

IN THE PREVIOUS CHAPTER, contemporary literature which exposits the distinction between law and gospel was reviewed and examined. In light of these various proposals surrounding this integral Lutheran distinction, the following research question is now addressed: *What are the scriptural and theological foundations for the distinction between law and gospel in confessional Lutheranism?* These foundations must first be laid before an evaluation of the difference between the confessional Lutheran approach and that of Gerhard Forde can be made. Because the distinction between law and gospel lies at the heart of the theology of the Lutheran Reformation, numerous writings that explain this topic have been published since the sixteenth century. A variety of sources are used in this chapter to expound upon this important topic. Most central here are the Lutheran Confessions themselves. These documents lie at the epicenter of the Lutheran tradition and lay the theological foundation upon which all other writers build. Alongside these confessional documents, several writers who have been influential within the development of the Lutheran tradition will be cited, including Martin Chemnitz and Johann Gerhard. These two writers are determinative of the theology which developed in the Protestant scholastic era that Gerhard Forde criticizes. In addition to these writers, the American Lutheran theologian Francis Pieper's *Christian Dogmatics* is referenced, as this is a foundational textbook from which modern writers largely base their own discussions on the topic. Contemporary literature is also utilized throughout this chapter to demonstrate the conclusions of modern scholarship on the law-gospel distinction in view of the traditional Lutheran position.

Definition of the Law

Among confessional Lutheran theologians, it is acknowledged that there are numerous ways in which the term νόμος is used throughout the New Testament, as well as *torah* in the Old, and there are, for that reason, a number of correct renderings of the term "law." There is a *general sense* in which the word *lex* or "law" refers to the entirety of Christian doctrine. Gerhard notes that this is the sense which often occurs in the Psalms, wherein the psalmist desires to explain the entirety of Yahweh's message through use of the language of law, such as in Ps 19:7–8.[1] In this way, the language of law is actually a synecdoche for both law and gospel. Chemnitz, similarly, describes this general sense and speaks of it as God's teaching which has been "universally revealed."[2] This is not, however, how the term is usually and properly used in a theological sense.

Along with this general sense, there are a number of other ways in which the language of law is used in the biblical text. Sometimes, the law is used as a power or force, as in Rom 7:25. Chemnitz refers to this as the *general sense*, whereas Gerhard denotes it as a use of *metonymy*. "Law" often refers to books of Scripture, either the entire Old Testament, or the five books of Moses in particular. Texts such as John 10:34 demonstrate that the Psalms, along with the books of Moses, are described as law. Chemnitz notes that the Old Covenant is referred to as law when it is contrasted with the superiority of the New Covenant.[3] Gerhard further outlines a number of senses of the term which he describes as *secondary*, including the customs of Gentile nations, general positive instruction, and human law as opposed to divinely ordained law.[4] It is important to note all of the various senses in which the Lutheran tradition has recognized that the biblical category of law is utilized, because when examining the biblical text, the Lutheran Reformers were well aware of the multifaceted nature of biblical terms. None

---

1. Gerhard, *On the Law*, 4.
2. Chemnitz, *Loci Theologici* 2:592.
3. Ibid., 2:593.
4. Gerhard, *On the Law*, 5–6.

of these are, however, what the Lutheran Reformers meant when speaking of the law in its *proper* sense, or of the law in distinction from the gospel.

It is noteworthy that the Lutheran tradition has acknowledged the multifaceted nature of the language of law in light of some modern critiques of the Lutheran view. Reformed theologian John Frame, for example, portrays the Lutheran perspective as if the only function of the law in the Lutheran tradition is its condemnatory power upon the sinner.[5] In contrast to this, he notes that the language of "gospel" in Scripture often has commandments attached to it, and similarly, law terminology is not always utilized in reference to a negative action of God upon the sinner. Such a reading of the Lutheran sources is a caricature of the perspectives explained by Chemnitz, Gerhard, and the rest of the Lutheran tradition. These simplistic critiques of the law-gospel distinction do not account for the highly nuanced arguments of Lutheran orthodox theologians who consistently express the fact that the concepts of both law and gospel are utilized in a variety of senses by the biblical authors.

The clearest definition of the law within the confessions is found in Article V of the Solid Declaration, under the heading of "Law and Gospel." In this section, a number of essential points about the nature of the law are addressed which are determinative for the development of the doctrine of law in the later Lutheran tradition. The Formula distinguishes a broad use of the term "law," as do the later dogmaticians, but speaks specifically in this article about how the law is defined *proprie* (FC SD V.17). In this proper sense, the law is described as the *immutabilis Dei voluntas*. The law is thus unchanging and is a reflection of God's own moral nature and character. It is eternal, and thus cannot be limited simply to mean "that which accuses," as Forde contends. There is a distinction made in the Formula between the essence of the law, as that eternal divine will, and the *office* of the law. The *officium* of the law is explained in a twofold manner: it "reprove[s] sins and teach[es] concerning good works" (FC SD V.18). This distinction between the law's essence and office is essential. Condemning is simply the *officium* of the law, and due only to the presence of sin. Law is eternal, and thus exists apart from its condemning function. It is also noteworthy that the office of the law is not limited to its condemning power, but includes instruction unto good works.

The late sixteenth-and seventeenth-century Lutheran dogmaticians, following the Formula of Concord, likewise define the law as the eternal

---

5. Frame, *Systematic Theology*, 96–97.

moral will of God. Chemnitz echoes Melanchthon's definition, by defining the law as "eternal and unmovable," reflecting God's own nature, and thus binds all people to obedience.[6] The obedience unto which one is bound is not simply external actions, but the movements and motivations of one's heart. Gerhard gives a rather simple, yet concise, definition of the law as "The rule of what should be done and what should be avoided."[7] The scholastics follow Aquinas in his threefold division of the Old Testament law as moral, civil, and ceremonial. In a general sense, all of these are law, or rules, given by God for men to follow. Yet, "*most specifically*," the law is a reference particularly to the moral law as exposited in the Ten Commandments.[8]

This threefold division of the law allows theologians to continue to promote the Decalogue as a reflection of God's eternal and immutable will, while recognizing the temporal nature of the other Old Testament commandments. Chemnitz outlines four arguments demonstrating that this threefold distinction has biblical precedent.[9] First, there are texts in the Old Testament, such as Deut 6:1, where a distinction is made between laws and ceremonies. The laws, according to Chemnitz, are moral precepts, whereas ceremonies include civil and ceremonial commands. Second, the means by which God gave the Ten Commandments differs greatly from the manner in which he gave the rest of his commands to the people of Israel. The Ten Commandments were written by the very hand of God, and placed on tablets which were to be kept in a sacred space. The Decalogue, unlike the ceremonial laws, was spoken directly to the people after Moses received it. Third, there are several passages which speak of the ceremonial and civil laws being given *specifically* to the people of Israel, and are thus not universal in nature. Finally, throughout the Gospels, Jesus promotes the moral law rather than the ceremonial or civil. This continuous attempt to distinguish between the three divisions of the Mosaic law differentiates Chemnitz from some later Lutheran theologians. If such a division exists, then Hofmann's contention that the entire law is simply one aspect of redemptive history that has been superseded is unfounded.

The moral law, according to confessional theologians (and the Ten Commandments in particular), existed prior to Sinai, and continues to do so after the fulfillment of the Old Covenant. Summarizing the developments

---

6. Chemnitz, *Loci Theologici* 2:598.
7. Gerhard, *On the Law*, 4.
8. Ibid, 5.
9. Chemnitz, *Loci Theologici* 2:613–14.

of the Lutheran scholastics, Schmid notes that the moral law was first given not at Sinai, but at the moment of creation.[10] Adam and Eve had the moral law both externally and in the heart. In the post-lapsarian state, the essence of the moral law remains and is imperfectly known through the conscience. This is referred to as the "*Law of Nature*."[11] Chris Vlachos has demonstrated that this creational perspective on the law is exegetically grounded. In his modified doctoral dissertation titled *The Law and the Knowledge of Good and Evil* (2009), Vlachos demonstrates that Paul grounds the law in the Edenic narrative and does not limit the divine commandments to the Sinaitic revelation. Through an examination of 1 Cor 15:56 and the Adam-Christ parallel in Rom 5, he argues that Paul connects sin, death, and law with the sin in Eden. Particularly noteworthy is the Pauline comparison between the age of Adam and Moses as that in which law was given (Rom 5:13–14). The Lutheran orthodox were not, then, simply reading their own theological presuppositions surrounding the divine law into the text, but argued in a manner consistent with at least one strand of Pauline scholarship.

For the Lutheran orthodox, the law was not given in an external and concrete manner between Eden and Sinai. Due to the effects of sin upon the mind and conscience, the human creature no longer was able to perfectly understand the moral demands of God. It was for this reason that God gave the moral law externally through the Ten Commandments on Mount Sinai. Hollaz states that this primordial law which existed prior to the fall does not differ in substance from the Sinaitic law; it differs only in the precise mode of revelation.[12] This is why Gerhard refers to the Ten Commandments simply as a repetition of the law, rather than the giving of new commands.[13] Chemnitz argues at length that each of the Ten Commandments was specifically explained prior to the Exodus.[14] He argues, for example, that the sixth commandment was clearly explained in the garden through the nature of the covenantal union of man and wife. Similarly, the seventh commandment is assumed when Adam is given work to perform in Eden. While modern interpreters will likely question some of Chemnitz's exegetical conclusions, his attempt to find such commandments in the Edenic narrative demonstrates just how important it was to him that

10. Schmid, *Doctrinal Theology*, 509.
11. Ibid., 509.
12. Ibid., 513.
13. Gerhard, *On the Law*, 28.
14. Chemnitz, *Loci Theologici* 2:632–34.

the Ten Commandments are not simply an aspect of one particular era of redemptive history, nor are they to be superseded eschatologically by something else.

The moral law, as revealed on Mount Sinai, includes both positive and negative commandments. Each is included within the other. When a negative commandment is given, a positive is to be inferred from its opposite.[15] These commandments require both outward and inward obedience. Though in its civil use, the law functions in restraining outwardly evil deeds, the law, in its fullest sense, condemns even the minor sins of the heart. Gerhard notes that the first commandment is included within the other nine commandments, so that in each, a perfect devotion to God is required.[16] Thus, if a person chooses not to commit the act of adultery, but only does so out of the fear of receiving the consequences of such an act rather than a pure love for God, then that person still violates the sixth commandment. Gerhard further demonstrates this fact by pointing out that the last two of the Ten Commandments reference the attitude of one's heart. This should not be read in such a way as to imply that it is only these two commands which relate to the condition of one's affections; the rest of the commandments must be read in light of these in accord with Jesus' exposition of the law in the Sermon on the Mount.[17]

Though the law existed in the primordial state apart from sin, and will continue to exist in the eschatological state without the threat of punishment, Lutheran dogmaticians have often included within the definition of the law its nature in the post-lapsarian creation. Chemnitz, in particular, emphasizes this fact, as he argues that one definition of the law is in "opposition to grace."[18] He further outlines this usage of the language of law in three points. First, the law does not approve partial obedience, but binds one to keep each of its precepts. The obedience demanded is both perfect and perpetual. Second, the law promises eternal life, but only to those who have perfectly followed its precepts. Deviation from even one divine command cuts one off from eternal life. Third, the law is harsh in its condemnation. There is no mercy in the law. It promises only punishment to those who disobey. It is this sense of the law, in contrast to the gospel, which

---

15. Gerhard, *On the Law*, 55.
16. Ibid., 56.
17. Ibid.
18. Chemnitz, *Loci Theologici* 2:593.

is most often used in Lutheran discussions surrounding the relationship between God's two words.

In summary, the Lutheran dogmaticians are careful to define "law" in a multitude of ways in accord with the biblical witness, as well as the various states in which the human race lives. At times, the law is simply instruction, or in its broadest sense, Scripture. Most often, however, the law refers to God's eternal and immutable will. The law is then an aspect of God's own nature, and not simply a condemning force toward the sinner. The sinner is condemned not because condemnation is of the essence of the law itself, but because of the inconsistency between the sinner and God's own holiness as expressed in the divine precepts.

Definition of the Gospel

Like the term "law," the word "gospel" has been used in a number of different senses throughout history. The confessional Lutheran tradition has recognized this variety of uses, but restricts its meaning in the proper theological sense. These broader senses must first be explained before the term in its most particular theological sense can be expounded.

Chemnitz has a detailed discussion of the etymology of the term "gospel," which helps lay a backdrop for its more particular theological application. He notes that the term *euangelizesthai* in the Septuagint is in view when the New Testament authors utilize the same concept. According to Chemnitz, this term is not used *generally* in the Old Testament for any type of good news, but it is restricted to contexts in which one is liberated from enemies and granted peace.[19] This liberation from enemies serves as a picture of the liberation won by Christ for the people of God. In other texts, the term "gospel" is used prophetically, in reference to the work of Christ in the new covenant. This has specific reference to the fact that this news is meant for the Gentiles as well as the Jewish people.

Because of the reality of Gentile inclusion in the new covenant, Chemnitz argues that the New Testament authors draw not only from the Old Testament, but also from common Greek speech when using the term "gospel." He states that there are three meanings assigned to this term in ancient Greek writers, which informs its use by the New Testament authors. First, it is used in the context of a good announcement, especially when proclaiming that a military victory has been won. Second, it is used as a synecdoche

---

19. Ibid., 819.

to refer not to the news itself, but to a gift given to the messenger of this good news. Third, it is utilized (again as a synecdoche) to describe sacrifices and prayers offered by those who have received the good news.[20] Chemnitz argues that all three of these meanings are in accord with its biblical usage. The pagan utilization of this term helps to explain why it is the term "gospel" rather than "law" which is used as descriptive of the new covenant. As demonstrated above, the term "law" can, at times, be used to designate that which is properly the gospel. However, the language of law might appear restrictive to the Jewish people; the term "gospel" assures that this concept is universally understood and applied. Furthermore, the terms are distinguished so that the New Testament writers have a means of distinguishing Moses from Christ, and God's commandments from his promises.[21]

Similarly, Article V of the Formula of Concord discusses the broad nature of the language of "gospel" within the biblical text. The Formula states that there are primarily two ways in which the term "gospel" has been used in theology as well as in Scripture. First is the *"generalis . . . definitio,"* which comprises the gospel in its widest sense, simply as the teachings of Christ (FC SD V.5). This is reflected in the designation of the four canonical books surrounding the life of Christ as "Gospels." These works are designated as such due to their emphasis on the life and teachings of Christ. When used in this broad sense, "gospel" refers to both commands and promises. This is sometimes done, more specifically, as one distinguishes between the Old Testament as "law" and the New as "gospel." In its most proper sense, however, the gospel must be distinguished from the law, and refers specifically to the promises of God as found in Christ.

The Lutheran confessional tradition defines the gospel in terms of both its content and its effects. Article V of the Formula, *"De Lege et Evangelio,"* arose out of a conflict surrounding the purpose and use of the gospel in preaching. Following Johann Agricola, a group of theologians had argued that there is no need to preach the law to Christians. Christian preaching, properly, consists solely in the gospel, which includes repentance. Luther himself argued against this position prior to his death, labeling these theologians "antinomian." Article V seeks to address this issue by explaining the nature of both the law and the gospel. If the gospel includes repentance, then the narrow definition of the law as defended by the Reformers was in error. In contrast to this, the Formula defines the gospel in its proper sense

20. Ibid., 820.
21. Ibid., 819.

thus: "For everything that comforts, that offers favor and grace of God to transgressors of the Law, is, and is properly called, the Gospel, a good and joyful message that God will not punish sins, but forgive them for Christ's sake" (FC SD V.21). The gospel is distinctively different from the law, not only in its content, but also in its effects. When defined in its most particular theological sense, the gospel is *only* good news; it does not bring about repentance or give commands to the believer.

While the confessions emphasize the impact of the gospel upon sinners, it is not *only* defined by its effects. The Lutheran confessional tradition has argued that the gospel is something objective which has particular theological content attached to it. Faith in Christ is not faith in the abstract, but in the particular historical person of Jesus, along with a number of convictions surrounding his atoning work. In particular, this includes faith in the *satisfactio vicaria*. Chemnitz outlines seven specific benefits of redemption which lie at the center of the gospel. First, Christ made satisfaction to the Father by his atoning death. Second, Jesus actively fulfilled God's law so that his righteousness might be granted to them that believe. Third, the benefits of Christ, including both his active and passive obedience, are received solely by faith. Fourth, God works his forgiveness through the means of grace: word and sacrament. Fifth, the gospel includes the promise of the Holy Spirit, through whom the believer's will and affections are changed. Sixth, the gospel includes the eschatological hope of eternal life. Finally, these promises are universal in scope, and pertain to the entirety of the human race.[22] Chemnitz warns that when any of these seven elements of the gospel is discarded, the doctrine of justification itself will likely be lost. Because of his insistence both on the fact that the gospel is truly news, which contains a number of specific theological propositions, and that the gospel can be explained in terms of its effects (those being the forgiveness of sins and the comforting of the conscience), it can be rightfully said that Chemnitz understands the gospel as both the *verba Dei* and *opera Dei*. When explicating the gospel as a separate *locus*, it is explained in *verba Dei* terminology, but when contrasted with the law, Chemnitz emphasizes the gospel's existential effect upon the human creature.

In its very essence, the gospel includes both *historia salutis* and *ordo salutis* realities. In one sense, the language of gospel specifically references the objective actions of Christ in history. This encapsulates the reality of Christ's active obedience, passive obedience, and resurrection from the

22. Ibid., 828.

dead, as St. Paul uses the term "gospel" in 1 Cor 15:3–8. Pieper refers to this historical sense of the gospel as "objective reconciliation."[23] This is the fact that Christ won reconciliation for the entire human race through his death and resurrection. This occurs prior to, and apart from, the personal act of faith. In Christ's resurrection, all people have been declared righteous through a universal absolution placed upon humanity. In this sense, the gospel is not an existential reality at all, but a historical fact. This is not the *only* way in which the gospel must be exposited, however. The gospel does not remain simply an objective reality out there in the realm of past history, but arises within the context of particular individuals. Through the giving of the gift of faith via regeneration, the objective reconciliation won by Christ is subjectively applied to the individual. Pieper argues that justification (both objective and subjective) is the central doctrine of the Christian religion,[24] and that it is synonymous with the gospel itself.[25] With the doctrine of objective and subjective reconciliation, the *essentia* and *officium* of the gospel are united in one concrete reality.

The distinction between objective and subjective justification helps to mitigate some criticisms leveled against the Lutheran perspective on the gospel. Lane Tipton, professor of systematic theology at Westminster Seminary in Philadelphia, has argued that the Lutheran tradition is myopically focused on one individual point of Christian theology to the neglect of other central biblical themes.[26] Tipton argues that there are two primary problems with the contention that justification is the central doctrine of the Christian religion. First, this privileges the *ordo salutis* over the *historia salutis*. The personal application of salvation through justification has a theological priority over the actual accomplishment of salvation in the life and death of Christ. For Tipton, the Lutheran tradition privileges the third article of the creed over the second. To defend this assertion, Tipton cites Pieper, who contends that all Christian theology finds its apex in the doctrine of justification. The problem with Tipton's argument is that he fails to understand Pieper's distinction between objective and subjective justification. For Pieper, the phrase "justification" references both an *ordo salutis* and *historia salutis* reality. The centrality of justification in the

---

23. Pieper, *Christian Dogmatics* 2:347.
24. Ibid., 512.
25. Ibid., 545–48.
26. Tipton, "Union with Christ," 42–45 in Oliphant, *Justified in Christ*.

Lutheran orthodox tradition, then, emphasizes *both* realities as central. Neither stands without the other.

Tipton's second criticism of the gospel in the Lutheran tradition is that the application of the gospel is limited primarily to a discussion of justification as a singular aspect of the *ordo salutis*. In doing this, Lutheran theologians make other important elements secondary such as union with Christ, sanctification, and regeneration. Tipton concludes that in Lutheranism, "justification is a bare declarative act that occurs outside of or prior to union with Christ."[27] For the Reformed tradition, union with Christ centralizes all benefits of salvation within itself, so that the *ordo* does not include a series of unconnected acts, with the center being the legal declaration of justification. Three points are to be made in response to this criticism. First, when Lutheran theologians argue that subjective justification precedes union with Christ, they are referencing the mystical union specifically, which consists in the indwelling of the Triune God. That does not mean, however, that there is no sense in which a kind of union precedes justification. Pieper himself acknowledges this, though in a footnote which might be easy to miss. In his definition of faith, Pieper notes that one synonym of faith is "joining oneself" to Christ.[28] He then adds a footnote to this definition with the statement that there is a kind of union which *logically* precedes subjective justification, which is an external union that occurs in faith. This idea, labeled the *unio fidei formalis*, comes from David Hollaz. Thus Tipton's criticism that a Lutheran view of justification is divorced from Christ himself is mistaken. Second, the connection between the various elements of the order of salvation need not be a moment in the *ordo* itself, but the unity is found in the *historia salutis* reality of objective justification, upon which salvation is grounded. Third, Tipton assumes that justification is a one-time event in the *ordo salutis* which corresponds solely to the legal reality of the forensic declaration that one is righteous. In the Lutheran orthodox, justification is not a one-time moment in the order of salvation, but it is a continual and repeated reality. Also, though justification is itself a legal act, it is intimately tied to the other biblical metaphors regarding salvation, such as adoption (which many Lutheran orthodox argue is a part of justification itself), sanctification, and regeneration.

As with "law," the confessional Lutheran tradition recognizes the variety of uses that the term "gospel" has in Scripture. In essence, these different

---

27. Ibid., 45.
28. Pieper, *Christian Dogmatics* 2:434.

permutations can be narrowed down to two: a wide and a narrow sense. In the wide sense, the gospel refers to the whole teaching of Christ, but in the narrow sense, it refers to God's promise of salvation in Christ. This narrow sense is further broken down into two specific parts: the essence of the gospel in history (objective reconciliation), and the effect of the gospel in the individual (subjective justification). These distinctions between the law and the gospel help to explain how these two words differ, as well as cohere with one another.

Contrast and Continuity between Law and Gospel

An examination of the definitions of both law and gospel in their proper theological sense demonstrates several areas of continuity and discontinuity between them. Due to the predominance of the law-gospel paradigm in Lutheran theology, particularly as these two ideas are heavily distinguished from one another, one might get the impression that these two words are contradictory. In the confessional Lutheran tradition, however, these two words are not incongruous. Instead, they simply represent different aspects of the one unified will of God for the salvation of sinners. In this section, the similarities and areas of continuity between law and gospel will first be examined, followed by an explication of the ways in which the law and the gospel differ from one another.

In Chemnitz and Gerhard, separate sections treat both law and gospel. Chemnitz, in his *Loci Theologici*, separates his treatment of the law and of the gospel by four other unrelated topics. There is thus no unified treatment of "law and gospel." Gerhard has two separate volumes on law and gospel respectively, with his volume on the gospel following that on the law. In the high scholastic era, with the writings of Abraham Calov, Johannes Quenstedt, and David Hollaz, law and gospel are treated together as a separate locus. This is usually included within a broader discussion of the means of grace which contains the topics of the word of God, baptism, and the Lord's Supper. The distinction between law and gospel is treated as the central aspect of God's word as a means of grace. Within this treatment of law and gospel, dogmaticians generally include a discussion of the commonalities between law and gospel, as well as the disparities between the two words of God. Such a discussion was generally followed by early confessional theologians in America, including Conrad Lindberg, Henry Eyster Jacobs, Adolf Hoenecke, and Francis Pieper. Of these treatments of this issue, Pieper's argument is the most extensive, and thus will serve as the primary basis to explain the contrast and continuity between law and gospel in the confessional Lutheran tradition.

Though Pieper spends a larger amount of space discussing the discontinuity between God's commands and promises than the continuity, he believes that there are several ways in which these two doctrines cohere with one another. The first point of continuity that Pieper gives is that both law and gospel have the same source.[29] Both the law and the gospel are words which arise from the mouth of God and are contained in Holy Scripture. Though it may be true that the gospel is, in some sense, a "higher word" than the law, one is not less inspired than the other. Pieper is firmly committed to the scholastic perspective on the verbal inspiration of Scripture and makes an exact identification between Scripture and the word of God. This being the case, all that is contained in Scripture, including God's promises *and* commands, is inspired and inerrant. Any hermeneutic which privileges gospel sections of Scripture as somehow more inspired than the rest of the text is rejected as inconsistent with verbal inspiration. This idea is contrasted by Scott Murray with the Valparaiso theologians, who promoted a gospel-reductionism, wherein the gospel sections of Scripture have a higher authority than expositions of God's law.[30] Pieper's conviction, in view of his perspective on biblical inspiration, that both of these words are divine, serves as a basis through which he explores the further connection between these doctrines.

The second point of continuity between law and gospel, according to Pieper, is that they are both universal in nature.[31] Writing in the largely Calvinistic context of nineteenth-through early twentieth-century American theology, Pieper writes, throughout his *Christian Dogmatics*, about the necessity of *gratia universalis* in opposition to the particular and limited grace proposed by Reformed theologians. God's saving will is universal, and the intent of Christ's atoning work is also universal. Due to his contention regarding the comprehensive effects of original sin and his commitment to universal grace, Pieper is insistent that God intends both his words of law and gospel to impact all sinners. In a Reformed context, the law is universal in scope, but the gospel (though universal through the supposed "outward call") is only earnestly intended for the elect. It is the Reformed

---

29. Pieper, *Christian Dogmatics* 3:224.
30. Murray, *Living God*, 92–100.
31. Pieper, *Christian Dogmatics* 3:224.

writer, then, rather than the Lutheran, who differentiates between the *telos* of the law and the gospel. In Lutheran confessional theology, the ultimate goal of God's word of law is that one might be convicted and driven to the salvation promised in the gospel. For the Calvinist, this is only the case for the elect. God's ultimate *telos* regarding the reprobate is for their eternal damnation in order that God might glorify himself through the outpouring of divine wrath.

Some contemporary Reformed theologians, such as R. Scott Clark and Michael Horton, have argued that the Reformed tradition has held to a strong law-gospel distinction in the same manner as the Lutheran Reformation. Horton uses the law-gospel distinction throughout his systematic theology *The Christian Faith*, and Clark similarly speaks in this manner in *Recovering the Reformed Confessions*. The vast discontinuity between these two traditions surrounding the *telos* of the law, however, demonstrates that while some similarities exist, these two traditions do not speak with a unified voice on the subject of law and gospel. Furthermore, these Reformed writers explain the distinction between God's two words through the context of covenant theology, wherein God's law corresponds to the covenant of works (given in Eden and republished at Sinai) and the gospel to the covenant of grace (given in the Abrahamic, Davidic, and new covenants).[32] Lutherans never developed this type of system, and place the law-gospel distinction in the context of God's speech, rather than his establishment of two overarching biblical covenants. There is then no common law-gospel distinction between the Calvinistic and Lutheran traditions. Some Reformed theologians criticize Lutheranism for its supposed emphasis on

---

32. There is a significant amount of debate within the Reformed community surrounding the precise nature of covenant theology. Some have argued against the entire bi-covenantal system, and argue instead that there is only one covenant, extending from Eden through the new covenant. This position, known as mono-covenantalism, is taught by Norman Shepherd, and was subsequently adopted by several writers in the Federal Vision movement. Within the more predominant bi-covenantal view, there are also several areas of debate. Most prominent among these, perhaps, is the idea of a republication of the covenant of works at Sinai. For a covenant theological perspective that affirms republication, see Michael Horton's book *Introducing Covenant Theology*. An alternative approach to covenant theology can be found in O. Palmer Robertson's *Christ of the Covenants*. The Orthodox Presbyterian Church recently published a report on the issue, in which certain strands of a republication perspective are rejected as inconsistent with the Reformed confessional documents.

discontinuity between law and gospel,[33] but it is ultimately the confessional Lutheran tradition which unites the two in God's universal saving will.

The final—and most important for Pieper—way in which the law and the gospel are commensurate is that both of these words of God are to be proclaimed from the pulpit.[34] Neither the law nor the gospel can be neglected prior to the Parousia. Pieper adamantly rejects Agricola's contention that the gospel is an instrument of both repentance and faith, thus negating the necessity of the law in the church. It is the law, not the gospel, which produces repentance, and the gospel then follows the law by granting faith to the contrite sinner. The law, like the gospel, is a necessary word for the believer, which continues its work in all three functions.

Along with these three ways in which law and gospel cohere with one another, Pieper argues that law and gospel are, in some sense, "perfect opposites."[35] These two words of God have dramatically different effects. The law demands, and the gospel gives. In a post-lapsarian situation, the law cannot grant life but only brings condemnation and death; to the contrary, the gospel does not condemn, but only brings life. As is apparent throughout Pieper's treatment, however, especially in light of his commitment to the doctrine of divine simplicity, it is not that the law and gospel contradict one another in their *essence*, but in their effect upon the human subject. Biermann criticizes what he calls a law-gospel polarity, which exposits the two words of God as contradictory, not just in terms of how the human subject perceives them, but in essence.[36] As will be demonstrated below, this is not Pieper's intention, although isolated statements might give such an impression.

In some sense, both the law and the gospel have conditions attached to them. Both of these words of God demand. The nature of these conditions and demands, however, differs. The law demands perfect obedience to all of its precepts. There are no loopholes around God's requirements in the divine law; one is bound to obey every element of the commandments without fail. The gospel demands only one thing, however: faith. Because the promises of God "frequently have the form of conditional statements,"[37] one can, in some sense, speak about faith as a condition for receiving the

---

33. For example, see the critique of John Frame cited above.
34. Pieper, *Christian Dogmatics* 3:224–27.
35. Ibid., 228.
36. Biermann, *Case for Character*, 116.
37. Pieper, *Christian Dogmatics* 3:230.

promises of the gospel. This is not to be understood, however, in the sense that faith is a human achievement which is deserving of God's promises. Instead, faith is a divine gift, and its conditionality is receptive in nature. The gospel does not demand faith as a good work, but as a means of clinging to its promises.

Along with their different conditions and demands, the law and gospel have different types of promises offered within them. The end goal of these promises is the same—eternal life—but the means of attaining this life differs. Lutheran dogmaticians have historically differentiated between *promissiones conditionales* and *promissiones gratuitae*. The law promises life to those who obey its demands, whereas the gospel promises life as a gift of pure grace. As stated previously, the gospel can in some sense be said to have "conditions" attached, but the gospel promises are not conditional in the *strict* sense, since God himself provides the necessary condition of reception. God grants the conditional promises in the law so that one might see one's inability to perform these actions and thus seek solace in the gracious promises found in the gospel.

Perhaps most importantly, the law and gospel differ in that the law always leads to the gospel. In this sense, the gospel is a "higher word" than the law.[38] Each of these doctrines has an important part in the economy of salvation and to the application of salvation to the individual in particular. As St. Paul argues in Romans, the gospel is the "end of the law" (Rom 10:4) for the believer. Regarding one's salvation, the gospel puts an end to the condemning voice of God's law. This does not mean that the law no longer functions in the life of the believer, since the Christian remains both saint and sinner until the eschaton. In fact, even when the believer no longer requires the prodding of the law in heaven, the law itself still remains as the eternal and immutable will of God. In an existential and soteriological sense, however, the law comes to an end through the proclamation of the gospel.

Due to Pieper's strong language of contrast between law and gospel, one might interpret him in such a manner as to infer a contradiction between the law and the gospel *essentially*, and as a proponent of the law-gospel polarity that Biermann criticizes. At one point Pieper argues, for example, that Hegelian theologians who seek to find a "higher unity" of law and gospel are in error.[39] This should not be read as if there is a complete

38. Ibid., 232.
39. Ibid., 250.

ontological divide between the law and the gospel, however. There are four aspects of Pieper's thought which demonstrate the contrary. First, Pieper acknowledges that there is a proper sense in which one can indeed speak of a higher unity of law and gospel which finds that unity in God himself.[40] Second, in Pieper's view, God is ontologically simple.[41] There is, in God, no distinction between essence and attribute, substance and accident. Thus, there are no distinctions, in an ultimate sense, between the attributes themselves. God is both wrath and grace, and these two aspects of his being are not opposed to one another, or even distinct. If God is simple, law and gospel simply *cannot* contradict one another. This is why Pieper ultimately confesses, "We fully realize that this does not explain how there can be both Law and Gospel simultaneously in God. But our limitation is due to the fact that our mundane knowledge bears the stamp: 'Now I know in part.'"[42] The contrast that law and gospel creates is not within God's own nature, but within the human creature. This is further demonstrated in the third point, that when speaking of their contrast, Pieper defines law and gospel in terms of their contradictory effects upon the sinner. He notes that he is not speaking of them as "abstract concepts" but specifically as addressed to individuals.[43] Finally, the discontinuity between law and gospel is ultimately reconciled through the *satisfactio vicaria*. In Pieper's view, it is necessary for Christ to fulfill God's demands on behalf of humanity, so that a perfect fulfillment of the divine law is imputed to those who believe. This final point will be addressed in detail below.

Though this discussion surrounding the contrast and continuity between law and gospel centers on one particular figure, Pieper's arguments here are consistent with the broader confessional Lutheran tradition. It is apparent that there is both contrast and continuity between law and gospel. They are consistent with one another in that they arise from the same source, they apply universally to all people, they share the same *telos* (the salvation of sinners), and both remain in the proclamation of the church until the eschaton. Discontinuities between law and gospel include different conditions, different promises, and different roles in the application of

---

40. Ibid.

41. The most extensive modern treatment of divine simplicity is James Dolezal's *God without Parts*. An extensive critique of divine simplicity has recently been published by Paul Hinlicky, titled *Divine Simplicity: Christ in the Crisis of Metaphysics*.

42. Pieper, *Christian Dogmatics* 3:235.

43. Ibid., 234.

salvation. These areas of discontinuity do not, however, refer to a contradiction between two different aspects of God's own nature, but to how these two distinct words impact sinful creatures. The continuity between law and gospel will be further developed through an examination of the traditional Lutheran perspective on the atonement.

Law, Gospel, and the Atonement

It is in the discussions surrounding the nature of the atonement in Lutheran orthodox theology that the continuity which exists between law and gospel is most clearly expressed. In the atonement, God's law and gospel meet one another, as Christ obeys the divine law on behalf of sinful humanity. Following his active obedience, Christ then dies a sinner's death as a substitute, paying the debt that all human creatures owe to their Creator due to the reality of sin. In these actions, God's law is fulfilled, and thus the gospel includes the perfect fulfillment of the divine commands. This concept will be discussed, first, in regard to Christ's active obedience, and second, in regard to his passive obedience.

There is no one explicit article in the Lutheran Confessions on the topic of atonement. The relevant ideas are, however, discussed under other headings—most commonly, justification. The third article of the Formula of Concord contains confessional statements surrounding both Christ's passive obedience and active obedience under the law. The specific topic under debate in this article is the connection between Christ's saving obedience and his two natures. This article is written to defend the notion that both Christ's divine and human natures are necessary for redemption, and functioned together in the work of atonement. There are, however, a number of assumptions underlying this article. First is the satisfaction theory of atonement. All parties in this debate agreed that Christ satisfied the demands of divine justice through his death on the cross; they disagreed over how that was done regarding Christ's divine nature. The language of *satisfactio* is used by the authors of the Formula to explain the efficacy of Christ's death (FC SD III.14–15). This satisfaction is specifically described as satisfaction *to the law* (FC SD III.15), which occurs *in our place*. The vicarious satisfaction atonement model is that of the Lutheran Confessions.

Although the Formula does not utilize the specific language of Christ's active and passive obedience, both realities are affirmed. An early Lutheran theologian, George Karg, argued that it is only Christ's death, not his life, that accounts for the sinner's justification. In opposition to this, the Solid Declaration affirms that Christ's substitutionary work does not refer only to his death, but also to his life of obedience to God's commands (FC SD III.15). Chemnitz further outlines this in his *Loci Theologici*. As a basis for his treatment of the active and passive obedience of Christ, he argues that God does not justify anyone apart from perfect righteousness. God's law is "eternal, immovable, and immutable."[44] Because of the law's eternal nature, its demands must necessarily be satisfied in order for God to vindicate the sinner. He asserts that "there can be no annulling, destroying, or doing away with the law."[45] There is thus a transfer of the law from the sinful creation to Christ. Chemnitz notes that there are two ways in which this is done. First, God removes the punishment of the law from humanity through Christ's substitutionary death; second, Christ perfectly obeys the divine precepts so that this obedience might be imputed to those who believe. Without using the later terminology of active and passive obedience, Chemnitz outlines the necessity of Jesus' fulfillment of both aspects of the law: its precepts and its curse.

The Lutheran scholastic tradition follows the Formula of Concord in affirming that the law must be fulfilled in order for God to declare the sinner righteous. The concepts of Christ's active and passive obedience are usually discussed under the heading "the office of Christ," and specifically in relation to his priestly office. This priestly office consists in Christ's intercession, death, and active obedience under the law. Heinrich Schmid, in his volume *The Doctrinal Theology of the Evangelical Lutheran Church*, outlines the seventeenth-century dogmatic teaching on atonement through a compilation of sections from Lutheran orthodox theologians. This work will be used to summarize the Lutheran consensus on this topic following the Formula of Concord. Schmid notes that satisfaction must be paid to God if sins are to be forgiven. It is inconsistent with the divine attributes, specifically justice and holiness, for God to pass over sin without punishment.[46] God's love and justice must work in accord with one another, so that God cannot love man and bring about salvation *without* the satisfaction of divine justice. Schmid argues that "something must first occur" for God to be enabled to be gracious unto sinful creation;[47] sin, by its very nature as

---

44. Chemnitz, *Loci Theologici* 2:1027.
45. Ibid., 1027.
46. Schmid, *Doctrinal Theology*, 343.
47. Ibid., 343.

opposition to the divine will, must be punished. The incarnation is thus not simply one option among many for man's redemption, but the only way in which human creatures could be reconciled to God. By taking upon himself a human nature, Christ placed himself as a substitute, being of the same essence as the race that he came to redeem. The divine nature of Christ is also a necessity for human redemption, because Christ's divinity grants an infinite worth to the punishment and merits of the finite human nature.

The two most important aspects of Christ's priestly work, according to the Lutheran orthodox, are his active obedience under the law and his passive obedience on the cross. Quenstedt notes that the distinction, though helpful, is not precise in explicating the difference between these two aspects of his work. There are certain aspects of the law that one must fulfill in which one is passive (circumcision, for example), but that is still reckoned as part of Christ's active obedience. Jesus was also not completely passive on the cross, but actively gave himself over to be crucified. Quenstedt points out that, in fact, it is really only the active obedience that is obedience in the proper sense at all. Only in a broader sense can Christ's death be called obedience to the law.[48] Yet, despite these qualifications, Quenstedt, Calov, Hollaz, and others in the scholastic tradition continue to utilize the distinction, while understanding the imperfection in terminology.

Schmid outlines three specific points as essential when explaining the active obedience of Christ under the law.[49] First, without the positive fulfillment of God's law in its entirety, God would be unable to forgive sinners. A salvation that includes *only* the passive obedience of Christ would be imperfect. Second, Christ was not subjected to the divine commandments on his own account; he submitted to the law purely for the benefit of his creation. Christ, as the eternal second person of the Holy Trinity, is Lord *over* the law, and thus has no obligation to place himself under it. This is true not only according to his divine nature, but also according to the human; this is an aspect of Christ's humiliation. Third, Christ obeyed the law as a substitute. He served in a representative fashion, as the second Adam, obeying the commandments of God in the place of the rest of humanity. Divine imputation is the end for which Christ's active obedience was rendered.

Christ's active obedience was to the entirety of the Mosaic law, including its moral, civil, and ceremonial aspects. Regarding the ceremonial

---

48. Ibid., 352.
49. Ibid., 352–53.

laws, Christ fulfilled it as the antitype who was portrayed by shadows in the various ceremonies God gave to Israel, such as the temple, sacrifices, the priesthood, and so forth. He also fulfilled the specific ceremonial requirements of the law in force in the first century, such as undergoing circumcision and dedication at the temple. The judicial laws were fulfilled insofar as Christ obeyed those commandments which relate to natural law and are observed by both Jews and Gentile nations. Finally, Christ obeyed God's eternal and immutable will as explained in the moral law. He did so, not in the manner that the scribes and Pharisees did (hypocritically), but according to the original divine intent of each commandment. Christ's obedience to all three aspects of the law is imputed to believers for righteousness.[50]

This point of the active obedience of Christ, in particular, has been challenged in recent years by a number of writers. Robert Gundry has argued that such a doctrine is based upon a misunderstanding of the Pauline text.[51] In traditional Reformation thought, faith saves, not because the act of belief is somehow meritorious, but because faith serves as a human means of grasping Christ's righteousness; this includes both his active and passive obedience. Gundry purports that the actual construction "justification by faith" in Rom 3 and 4 does not support the contention that faith is merely an instrumental cause of justification, but that God actually declares faith itself to be righteous; there is no transfer of the righteousness of God (or of Christ, more specifically) to the sinner. John Piper wrote a short volume titled *Counted Righteous in Christ* in response to Gundry in defense of the traditional Reformation position on the topic. While perhaps not as convincing as one might hope, Piper does demonstrate that there are extensive exegetical grounds for the Reformation teaching surrounding Christ's obedience as the content of the sinner's righteousness *coram Deo*. This was followed by Brian Vickers, who wrote a doctoral dissertation on imputation and Christ's obedience in response to Gundry and other critics. In this work, Vickers demonstrates that Gundry and others have mistakenly attempted to prove, based upon the grammatical construction of a few texts in Romans and Galatians, that Christ's righteousness is not imputed to the sinner. He proposes that the proper manner in which to defend the doctrine of imputation, which includes the active obedience of Christ, is through a synoptic reading of various texts which relate to justification. In other words, one cannot prove the doctrine of Christ's active obedience

---

50. Ibid., 353.
51. Gundry, "Why I Didn't Endorse."

by one singular text—any more than one can do so for the doctrine of the Trinity or other orthodox teachings—but through a synthetic examination of various texts which speak about the issue. When this is done, a Pauline case for the imputation of Christ's righteousness, and consequently his active obedience, can be established. While contemporary Pauline scholarship is divided on the validity of the doctrine of active obedience, it has been demonstrated that a traditional Lutheran approach can still be ably defended by modern New Testament scholarship through a thorough examination of the biblical text.

Along with their convictions surrounding Christ's active obedience, the Lutheran orthodox also contended that salvation could not be accomplished *only* by Christ's active fulfillment of the law. The active obedience of Christ, without his passive satisfaction, could not save the human race. Along with positive righteousness, the guilt of sin must be taken away. This is done through Christ's death on the cross. The Lutheran tradition has historically utilized Anselmian language of satisfaction, though with some differences from the medieval theologian. Rather than divine honor needing satisfaction, God's justice and wrath must be satisfied through Christ's death. Gustaf Aulen contends that, on this point, the Lutheran orthodox depart from Luther himself, who utilized the *Christus Victor* motif rather than a legal model of atonement. While Aulen's contention that Luther rejected the Anselmian model remains unconvincing, he does demonstrate that the Reformer spoke in a variety of ways about the atonement and did not limit his own language to one particular model. On this point, the Lutheran orthodox were not wrong, or inconsistent with Luther, in writing extensively about the *satisfactio vicaria*, but a reliance on this one atonement model did result in a neglect of other valid atonement motifs. Despite these shortcomings, the scholastics expounded the satisfaction theory of the atonement in an extensively systematic and biblical manner. In explaining the nature of this satisfaction, Hollaz outlines two important aspects of what constitutes the *satisfactio vicaria*. First, "surrogation" is required, wherein a guilty charge against one person must be given to another. Christ took the guilty charge of the whole human race upon himself. Second, this guilty charge must be satisfied in such a way that it results in the release of the guilty party from punishment.[52] The only reason that such a transfer is possible is due to the dual nature of Christ, who takes sin upon himself

---

52. Schmid, *Doctrinal Theology*, 357.

as a man and constitutes the value of his substitutionary work as infinite according to his divine nature.

It is in the context of the atonement that the continuity between law and gospel is made clear. These two words of God do not contradict one another. Instead, the gospel includes the fulfillment of the law. In setting sinners free from the law's condemnation, God does not ignore his demands or excuse the sinner's lack of obedience. The gospel only has its power because of Christ's fulfillment of the law. The law *is* then in some sense a way to eternal life. According to Lutheran orthodoxy, from the writing of the Formula and Concord and forward, Christ obeys God's law as a substitute by his active obedience and his passive death on the cross. It is only when the law is fulfilled that God can remain both just and the justifier of the one who has faith.

The Third Use of the Law

An important teaching in Lutheran orthodoxy, which—alongside the vicarious atonement—emphasizes the essential goodness of the divine law, is the "third use" of God's commandments. The third use of the law, one of the most debated points in the contemporary Lutheran theological world, was not so controversial a teaching in orthodox Lutheranism following the Formula of Concord. There is a rather consistent teaching on this subject from the publication of the Formula of Concord onward within the Lutheran scholastic tradition. While the condemnatory aspects of God's law are central (in that due to its pedagogical nature, the law leads one to the gospel), this is not the *only* function of the divine law for the believer. It also serves in a positive manner, as a guide by which redeemed people are informed of the will of God. This will first be explored in the Formula of Concord, and then in the writings of Lutheran orthodoxy.

Following the death of Luther, there were a number of debates within the Lutheran church surrounding the nature of both the law and the gospel. One of these debates was centered on the "third use of the law" as promoted by Melanchthon and others. Luther himself, while certainly retaining a positive function of the law, did not speak explicitly of three distinct uses of the law. While the majority of early Lutherans were comfortable with Melanchthon's formulation, theology professor and co-author of the Formula of Concord Andreas Musculus was hesitant to speak about a third use of the law. He argued that Christian obedience is freely offered, not coerced.

In his perspective, the language of the law in its third use implied that the Christian's obedience is forced rather than spontaneous.[53] This controversy was settled in Article VI of the Formula of Concord, in favor of the third use, while addressing the concerns of Musculus.

The Formula outlines this issue by first addressing the agreement among all parties involved surrounding the first two uses of the law. In its first use, the law is an instrument of *disciplina externa* for those who are not regenerate (FC VI.1). In this sense, the law helps society to function properly. The second use of the law is the function of God's commands which demonstrate the reality of sin to the fallen creature. It is this use which leads to the gospel. It is also acknowledged that, among all parties, there is agreement that Christian obedience is wrought by the Holy Spirit, and this obedience is, according to the renewed man, spontaneous.

The side that is in favor of the third use of the law, which is defended by the Formula, argues that in their third function, the commandments serve as a "rule and standard of a godly life," and serve in a positive manner for the regenerate person (FC SD VI.3). This is because the law is a presentation of the *"immutabilem voluntatem Dei"* (FC SD VI.3); it is not merely a product of one particular period of redemptive history, or a set of temporary rules to be superseded at the eschaton. The law is as eternal as God himself, and since that is the case, the believer must always obey the divine commands, even apart from the reality of sin. This is further expressed with the contention that it is not the law itself, but the curse of the law which is removed from the believer. With the curse being removed, the Christian should still daily make effort to obey the commandments (FC SD VI.4).

Musculus's concerns are acknowledged in the Formula, as it is contended that the law should not be pushed upon believers as a burden. He was correct in emphasizing the reality that, according to the new man (the believer insofar as he has been renewed), the law is written on the heart. The necessity of the third use of the law is largely based on the now–not yet aspect of the Christian life. The believer is at once a product of the old age and of the new. According to the new man, no external study of the law is necessary, as the law itself is perfectly written on the heart. If the believer were to be freed from the old self, the law would no longer be necessary. This is not, however, the reality that Christians face. Along with the renewed self exists the old Adam. The believer is *simul iustus et peccator*. The Formula cites Rom 7 as the normative experience of the Christian life, wherein the

---

53. Arand, *Lutheran Confessions*, 198–99.

new and old natures are in a constant battle against one another (FC SD VI.8). One might get the impression, from all of this, that the law itself will no longer remain after the renewal of heaven and earth. For example, the Formula states that the believer, apart from sin, would "need no law" (FC SD VI.6). The point is not, however, that the law *itself* ceases to exist, but that its urgings upon the believer cease. This is demonstrated by the fact that the Formula states earlier that the law is eternal. This is further clarified by the connection made in this article between the Christian's obedience and the obedience of the rest of God's creation (FC SD VI.6). The Formula mentions the obedience rendered by the sun, moon, and stars as a parallel to the obedience rendered by Christians eschatologically. The heavenly bodies do not exist without law. In fact, they function with very particular scientific laws. Unlike the sinner, however, these objects do not need to be coerced into obedience. Like the rest of creation, after the resurrection, believers will simply do God's will without any coercion or force.

Following the division in the Formula, Chemnitz outlines and defends three uses of the law. The first use is the civil use, whereby the unregenerate person is constrained by the law; this occurs through the civil magistrate and natural law.[54] The second use, according to Chemnitz, is that which relates to justification. The law, in this sense, is a means whereby God condemns the sinner, leads him to despair, and prepares him for the gospel.[55] The third use, as explained by Chemnitz, is the law as it is necessary for those who are regenerate. He argues that this function of the law is a necessity in opposition to the Anabaptists. Many of the Anabaptists argued for the validity of their actions due to their conviction that such deeds were Spirit-led, even while disobeying God's revealed will. The third use of the law prevents enthusiasm, as well as man-made laws as were emphasized in the medieval church. The law thus keeps the Christian from basing moral decisions upon a whim which one feels is the Holy Spirit, or various traditions of the church; instead, these decisions can be made with certainty in accordance with God's revealed will.[56]

Chemnitz outlines two different aspects of Christian existence in relation to God's commandments. In one sense, the Christian is not under the law; in another, he is. Chemnitz names five specific features of the law which the Christian is *not* bound by: justification by it, its condemnation,

---

54. Chemnitz, *Loci Theologici* 2:805.
55. Ibid., 806–07.
56. Ibid., 807.

its accusation, its compulsion, and necessity for its perfect obedience.[57] In terms of its promise of eternal life through perfect obedience, the Christian is no longer under the law due to Christ's vicarious fulfillment of it. The Christian *is*, however, bound to obey God's law for the sake of love, as a rule whereby the regenerate person is guided in this life. Chemnitz outlines three particular aspects of the law which remain for the Christian while functioning in its third use. First, Christians are told exactly what forms of service God accepts so that they do not invent their own ideas about what God desires in worship and obedience. Second, the law stops Christians from becoming legalistic about their obedience. The law serves as a constant reminder of one's imperfections. Third, the law is necessary due to the sinful flesh that still remains in the Christian. Because of the old Adam, the Christian will *not* always obey God's law out of pure spontaneity. He is dragged down by the sinful inclinations of his heart, and the law is thus necessary to restrain evil. The law then works according to its "precepts, exhortations, warnings, and promises."[58] All of these aspects of God's law demonstrate that the law is a necessary tool in Christian obedience.

Chemnitz is concerned that when hearing the distinction between law and gospel taught in Lutheran theology, hearers will assume that obedience to God's commandments is unnecessary. Due to his convictions surrounding the third use of the law, Chemnitz corrects this by noting that though the law is impossible to fulfill in this life, one must not live a life of lawlessness and carnal security.[59] Though sin remains, every regenerate person will begin a life of obedience to God's commands. Chemnitz refers to this as "absolutely necessary."[60] He further connects faith with both justification and obedience. The same faith that receives Christ's righteousness also receives the Holy Spirit, who makes a beginning of good works in the life of all believers.

In Gerhard, following Chemnitz, the developed Lutheran perspective on the law in its third use is explicated. He, again, differentiates between the political, pedagogical, and didactic functions of the law. He repeats the contention from the Formula that due to the sinful nature, the divine law is a necessity for the Christian. However, he more strictly defines the third use of the law simply as that function of the law whereby the Christian is

---

57. Ibid.
58. Ibid., 808.
59. Ibid., 604.
60. Ibid., 605.

instructed in good works. He likens this to a bridle on a horse, which is used to stop the horse from going off of the correct path.[61] While Chemnitz speaks about the restraint and threats of the law in connection to the Christian's sinful flesh as an aspect of the third use of the law, Gerhard restricts that to the first use of the law.[62] In contrast to this, Chemnitz speaks of the first use as purely a civil function for the unbeliever. In substance, the views of Chemnitz and Gerhard are the same, as they both expound the necessity of the law for the believer both in its use as a guide for the regenerate, and to restrain the old sinful nature. Gerhard's language is more clear in differentiating these two functions, and was adopted by the scholastic tradition following him. This led to the now common categorization of the three uses of the law as curb, mirror, and guide.

It is a common assumption by non-Lutheran interpreters that the third use does not functionally exist within Lutheran thought. In the critique of John Frame mentioned previously, for example, it is argued that the law-gospel distinction cannot be correct due to the prologue of the Decalogue. In this instance, the gospel of redemption from Egypt precedes the giving of the specific commandments; this creates a gospel-law order rather than a law-gospel one. In other words, because the law in this instance is placed in the narrative as a response to divine grace, rather than an instrument of condemnation, the Lutheran view is incorrect. Frame also offers this critique in his more extensive treatment of law and gospel in his unpublished essay "Law and Gospel." In this article, Frame purports that the Lutheran view of the law's third use is simply the condemnatory use as applied to the Christian rather than the non-Christian. In this way, Frame has read the three uses of the law as simply various aspects of the *one* use of the law. In Frame's portrayal of Lutheranism, *lex semper accusat* is understood as *lex sola accusat*. Frame is not alone in such a characterization. Andrew Sandlin has argued similarly in his booklet *Wrongly Dividing the Word*, and Rich Lusk has echoed these same sentiments. For these authors, the simple fact that the Ten Commandments are rooted in the indicatives of God's redemption from Egypt negates the law-gospel distinction. As has been demonstrated through an examination of Chemnitz, Gerhard, and the Formula of Concord, this is based upon a complete misunderstanding of the law's third use.

---

61. Gerhard, *On the Law*, 224.
62. Ibid., 225.

Dean Wenthe explores this in his essay, "The Torah Story: Identity or Duty as the Essence of the Law,"[63] wherein it is argued that the law should not be divorced from its narrative context in the Mosaic account. Wenthe argues that the law is tied to the theme of identity for the people of Israel; God establishes the identity of the people of Israel through his unilateral act of grace consummated through Moses. The law then serves as a means by which the Israelites live out and express this identity through their obedience to the divine commands. Essentially, for Wenthe, the Sinaitic law was given in a third-use context, though this does not negate the other functions of the law throughout the Old Testament narrative. This is significant, because the author is a Missouri Synod Lutheran, and he does not see any conflict between the goodness of the law as God's guide to the redeemed people of Israel, and a strong distinction between the law and the gospel. Wenthe is not alone in his expression of the law in this manner. This essay was presented at the Symposium on Exegetical Theology at Concordia Theological Seminary in 2001, alongside other essays on this topic. Throughout these essays, collected in the volume *The Law in Holy Scripture*, the goodness of the divine law and its third function as a guide are continually exposited by a variety of Lutheran scholars. The problem, then, is not in Lutheranism's understanding of the law's third use, but in Frame's reading of Lutheranism.

While there are slight differences in terms of how the third use of the law is explained by Lutheran theologians, there is a unified testimony within the confessional Lutheran tradition surrounding the usefulness of the law for the believer. Though set free from the *condemnation* of the law, the believer is still under an obligation to obey its precepts. This is done not as a means to merit salvation, but as a response to justification by grace. The Ten Commandments, in particular, represent the immutable will of God, and thus are the design for which God has created his creatures. By the Spirit, all Christians begin to obey God's commands, though they will never do so perfectly in this life. Before the resurrection, the law guides believers, demonstrates their continual need for Christ, and keeps their sinful flesh restrained from gross outward sins.

---

63. In *Law and Holy Scripture*, 21–35.

The Scriptural Foundations of the Law-Gospel Distinction

As has been apparent throughout the study thus far, the confessional Lutheran tradition has always tied its theological convictions surrounding law and gospel to the biblical text. Luther himself arrived at his perspective on this subject through an examination of St. Paul's writings to the Romans and Galatians. Chemnitz and the other writers of the Formula of Concord were also concerned to defend this distinction exegetically, especially as they faced challenges from their Roman Catholic opponents. Though this study does not permit a full scriptural examination of the relevant texts, the most important biblical foundations for the law-gospel distinction in historic Lutheranism will be explained and examined.

It was made apparent above that the Lutheran orthodox sought to utilize the terminology of law and gospel in a biblical manner. The Formula of Concord, Gerhard, and other theologians recognize that there are a variety of ways in which the specific terms "law" (*torah* or *nomos*) and "gospel" (*euangelion*) are used throughout Scripture. Sometimes they are used as a synecdoche to refer to the entirety of the Christian message, and at other times they are terms for the distinction between the old and new covenants. Any attempt to critique the traditional Lutheran approach to the law-gospel distinction purely on etymological grounds is thus misguided. The type of critique offered by contemporary Reformed theologian John Frame (as cited previously), who notes that commandments are often connected to gospel terminology in the New Testament, is unconvincing.[64] In their broader senses, the law and gospel are not necessarily opposed to one another, and the type of observation made by Frame is thoroughly consistent with a Lutheran theological approach. Where the distinction between the law and the gospel *does* come from, however, is those particular passages which contrast God's commands and promises, especially in regards to justification.

In the Apology of the Augsburg Confession, Melanchthon argues that all of Scripture can essentially be divided into these two topics: law and gospel (Apol AC IV.5). He explicitly designates the law here as the Ten Commandments which are God's eternal will for all of creation, rather than the civil or ceremonial laws unique to the nation of Israel. This law is identical with natural law and can be partially explicated through reason alone as one examines natural revelation. The law consists in whatever is

---

64. Frame, *Systematic Theology*, 96–97.

a moral commandment, and the gospel he defines as "promises concerning Christ." These promises are either prophetic, in the Old Testament, or explicit, in the New Testament. Melanchthon's explanation serves to give a background to further explications of law and gospel from the biblical text.

The primary passages used by the Lutheran Reformers to defend the distinction between law and gospel are those texts from Romans and Galatians which attribute particular functions to God's law (namely, to condemn sin) and his gospel (namely, to bring salvation). These texts, along with others, will be briefly examined; first, regarding the law, and second, regarding the gospel. Chemnitz offers a thorough defense of this distinction in response to Rome's perspective on justification in his *Examination of the Council of Trent*. Throughout this section, he gives a summary explanation of the exegetical grounding for this distinction. This will serve as the basis for a brief examination of the exegetical foundation for the distinction between law and gospel in confessional Lutheran theology.

One of the primary points to be argued in Chemnitz's work is that the law requires complete and perfect obedience. When this obedience is rendered, the promise of eternal life is given to the one who obeys. This truth is grounded in a number of biblical texts which speak about God's commandments in this manner. Chemnitz argues synthetically, taking a number of texts on each topic and harmonizing them, as is the normal practice in scholastic theology. The contention that the law requires not simply partial, but perfect, obedience, and that such obedience is a condition for entering eternal life, is drawn from five particular texts.[65] First is Rom 2:13, wherein Paul writes that those who obey the law will be justified on the last day. This verse is heavily debated in contemporary Pauline scholarship, as it attributes justification not to faith, but to obedience to God's law. Some interpreters, such as N. T. Wright, have argued for a distinction between initial justification (by faith), and eschatological justification (by faith and obedience).[66] Others, such as Stephen Westerholm, have argued that this text presents a hypothetical scenario of salvation by obedience in order to demonstrate its impossibility in the next chapter.[67] The latter position is that of Chemnitz. In this perspective, Paul sets up the law as a means of salvation in Rom 2:13. This then serves as a background for the climax of his argument in 3:20 that, although the law offers salvation, no one has

---

65. Chemnitz, *Examination* 1:488–89.
66. Wright, *Apostle Paul*, 113–33.
67. Westerholm, *Lutheran Paul*, 268–73.

rendered the necessary obedience; all are thus condemned by the law as guilty. This is in preparation for Paul's proclamation of the gospel, wherein he demonstrates that salvation comes through the gospel, because in that gospel, Christ's righteousness (which consists in his perfect law-keeping) is revealed.

Other texts used by Chemnitz in connection with the idea that the law requires perfect obedience are Gal 3:10 and 3:12 and Jas 2:10 and 2:11. The two texts from Galatians are part of Paul's long argument surrounding justification by faith rather than works. In Chemnitz's interpretation of these texts, Paul is setting up the impossibility of salvation by the law through personal obedience by outlining the necessity of the *perfection* required by the Mosaic covenant. One must not simply obey some or most of the commandments, but *all* of the commandments. Such obedience is impossible for the fallen human creature. Both of the texts Chemnitz cites from James further demonstrate this point, as the apostle notes that even in breaking one commandment, the sinner is declared a lawbreaker. This then leads to the contrast Paul makes in Gal 3:12 between two different means of receiving salvation: faith and works. The law cannot save because it depends on doing rather than believing. Many contemporary interpreters who reject a traditional law-gospel distinction have argued against this understanding of Paul's argument. E. P. Sanders has proposed that Paul's citation of Deut 27:26 in Gal 3:10 has nothing to do with a concept of perfect obedience required in the law. Instead, believing that salvation is by virtue of faith in Jesus, rather than law, Paul simply looked for any verse in the Old Testament which backed up his point.[68] The reason why Deut 27:26 is used is due to the connection the author makes between "curse" and "law." The phrase "all" is merely incidental, and is not central to the Pauline argument. Chemnitz, holding to a stricter view of biblical inspiration than Sanders, believed that each word in this text was given by the inspiration of God's Spirit, and the phrase "all" is thus essential to Paul's argument; it is also consistent with that which is said about the law (in that it requires absolute perfection) elsewhere in the New Testament.

In connection with the belief that the law requires perfection and offers eternal life to those who obey its precepts, one must then demonstrate that since such obedience is impossible, it is granted through the gospel rather than the law. The Lutheran Confessions utilize a number of Pauline texts to demonstrate the principle of *sola fide* through the gospel, such as Rom

---

68. Sanders, *Paul and Palestinian Judaism*, 21.

3:24, 28; Eph 2:8; and 1 Cor 15:56 (Apol AC IV.73, 79). In these texts, an explicit contrast is made between the law and justification (gospel). In Rom 3:24, Paul states that it is by grace, through Christ's redemption, that one is justified. This is then set in contradistinction to the law in 3:28, wherein he argues that justification is received *apart* from the works of the law. Some contemporary authors, such as James Dunn, have argued that Paul is not, in this context, speaking about the law as God's moral commandments generally speaking.[69] As noted above, the Lutheran Confessions function with a particular definition of the law, which is called the eternal and immutable will of God. Dunn argues, to the contrary, that the Pauline definition of law is dependent upon Jewish identity. Paul is not arguing against salvation by works in a general sense, but by those works which explicitly identify the Jews as the unique people of God. These objections are not novel, but were heavily utilized in the Roman Catholic–Lutheran polemics of the sixteenth and seventeenth centuries.

Chemnitz cites the Roman Catholic apologist Andrada as making a similar argument to contemporary interpreters.[70] According to this theologian, the only works excluded from justification are ceremonial works. He draws here on the Thomistic distinction between the threefold aspects of the law as moral, civil, and ceremonial. According to Andrada, the moral law is necessary for justification, while the civil and ceremonial are not. Dunn and other contemporary interpreters generally reject this threefold distinction, but the argument itself remains essentially the same whether one refers to "ceremonial law" or law as "Jewish identity markers." In either approach, moral works in general are not excluded from justification. A number of criticisms have been leveled against this approach by Lutheran theologians through the last five centuries.[71] The first point is that there are three texts that appear in Paul's writings which exclude good works in general from justification without mention of "law" in particular. These three texts are Eph 2:8, Titus 3:5, and 2 Tim 1:9. Nothing in the context of these three Epistles would imply that Jewish boundary markers were a matter of discussion. For many proponents of the New Perspective on Paul, these texts do not have any significant part in the debate because these writers deny Pauline authorship of the Pastoral Epistles, and often Ephesians (N. T. Wright being the exception). They are thus simply early interpretations

---

69. Dunn, *New Perspective*, 121–40.
70. Chemnitz, *Examination*, I:527.
71. Such as in Chemnitz, *Loci Theologici* 3:991–1003.

of Paul's teachings and are not explanatory in expounding upon Paul's own thought. The difference between confessional Lutheran teaching and the New Perspective, then, is partially one of canon.

The other reason why Dunn's approach is to be rejected is that Paul himself portrays the law as something universal. In his examination of the extensive reality of sin, he writes not only about the *torah*, but the law written on the heart (Rom 2:14–15), which includes Gentile nations. This is why Paul's concluding statement regarding the function of God's law states that through the divine commandments, the "whole world" is held guilty before God. Were Paul simply speaking about Jewish boundary markers, this phrase would be nonsensical. Chris Vlachos further argues this point by demonstrating that in Paul's thought, the law is creational. Paul connects the law in Rom 5 with the pre-fall Adamic state (Rom 5:13).[72] It is the Edenic law which serves as the basis for its recapitulation in the Mosaic covenant. Vlachos echoes the concerns of Chemnitz and Gerhard here, who demonstrate that God's laws existed in the prelapsarian state. They are thus universal, not limited to the Jewish nation.

The Lutheran Reformers were thoroughly biblical in their utilization of law-gospel terminology. They were not using a foreign theological concept as a hermeneutic to interpret these passages, but took the distinction from the text itself. According to the Lutheran tradition, the law is the eternal and immutable will of God. It is not, then, simply the unique property of the Jewish nation. This moral law requires perfect obedience, which the human race, Jew and Gentile alike, have failed to render. They must then seek justification somewhere else: in the gospel. This promise is distinguished from the law, and is received solely by faith.

The Practical Use of the Law-Gospel Paradigm

The distinction between law and gospel was never propagated by Lutheran orthodoxy as simply a collection of intellectual propositions. Luther himself arrived at his view on these subjects through intense existential struggle, along with exegetical engagement. While the tradition that followed him utilized more systematic categories to explain these teachings than the Reformer did, his concern for the practical pastoral implications of the law-gospel distinction was never dismissed. Chemnitz, Gerhard, Pieper, Walther, and many others consistently demonstrate their concern for the

---

72. Vlachos, *Knowledge*, 131–74.

proper application of these two teachings within the context of pastoral ministry and personal piety.

One of the primary concerns for the Lutheran Reformers is that of the burdened conscience. As is well known, Martin Luther struggled with a burdened conscience, believing himself to be justified through his obedience. He knew that as an unrighteous sinner, he could never stand before a holy God without condemnation. He needed an alien righteousness. Philip Cary, in his article "Why Luther Is Not Quite Protestant," argues that these concerns led Luther to a different perspective on the Christian faith than Calvin and later Protestant theologians. Rather than on an inward experience of conversion, Luther founded his assurance upon the objective means of grace, which for Luther, delivers the gospel. Later Lutherans continued to speak in this pastoral manner. The law, by its nature after the fall, accuses, and if the law and the gospel are not properly distinguished, sinners will be pushed back on their own righteousness and face existential despair. One place where this concern is evident within the Lutheran Confessions is in the third article of the Formula. This section is written surrounding a controversy that arose through the teachings of Andreas Osiander. In contrast to the authors of the Formula, Osiander argued that the righteousness which justifies is not the external alien righteousness of Christ, but the indwelling of Christ's *essential* righteousness according to his divine nature alone.[73] The Reformers were concerned that such a contention was a confusion of law and gospel, of justification and sanctification. Henry P. Hamman notes that the primary two concerns in the Osiandrian controversy were the comfort of broken sinners and the honor of Christ as Savior.[74] The authors of the Formula argued that rather than pointing to the alien righteousness of Christ in the gospel, Osiander directed people instead to their own internal renewal, and thus to the law. This leads one to despair.

The Formula outlines the practical pastoral reasons why a proper exposition of the righteousness that avails before God is necessary (FC SD III.30). There are two primary concerns: First, it is essential that troubled consciences might have assurance of their salvation. If righteousness *coram Deo* is dependent upon any love or virtue within the sinner, then salvation is always in doubt. The believer's regeneration is always imperfect in this life, and thus it cannot serve as a basis by which one determines the state of his or her soul (FC SD III.28). Faith rests in that which is perfect, namely,

---

73. Preus, *Contemporary Look*, 138–43.
74. Ibid., 146.

the external righteousness and merit of Christ that is apprehended by the sinner (FC SD III.IV). It is necessary that justification be spoken of in a forensic sense, as a divine declaration, lest human works be confounded with justifying righteousness. This, according to Biermann and Arand, is one of the most significant reasons why the two kinds of righteousness is a useful theological paradigm in expositing Lutheran theology. The second concern in the Formula is that the proper honor be given to God, who secures salvation for the sinner. The *sola gratia* principle leads to the doxological phrase "*soli Deo gloria*." If salvation is, in any sense, the work of the sinner through internal renewal, which the believer cooperates in, then glory is taken from God and placed onto the human creature. The manner in which one understands law and gospel, then, is essential to how one thinks about Christian worship. None of these concerns negate the correct understanding of the believer's inward renewal and activity of obedience. These realities are an essential aspect of the Christian life, as is the continuing function of the law. They must not, however, be conflated with justifying righteousness (FC SD III.39).

While the comfort of the troubled conscience is an essential aspect of the practical theology involved in the law-gospel distinction, the confessional Lutheran tradition is also concerned with the nature of preaching to the impenitent. While the contrite sinner is to be pointed to the gospel, the unrepentant sinner who uses the grace of God as an excuse for licentious living is to be pointed, instead, to the law. The gospel is never to be used as an excuse for the impenitent. Article IV of the Formula, on good works, argues that the believer's good deeds are necessary for the life of faith, though not for salvation (FC SD IV.14). This is to be preached against the "Epicurean delusion" (*Epicureae opinionem*) that one can retain true faith and live in open sin (FC SD IV.15). There is such a thing as a "dead faith," wherein one professes to trust in Christ while simultaneously living without repentance and good works. Though Christians struggle against sin, they do not intend to live in persistent sin, and daily repent of their shortcomings. If this continual repentance is not present in a person, that individual is to be treated as an unbeliever, and the law, rather than the gospel, is to be proclaimed.

Another concern regarding the distinction between law and gospel is that the Christian faith be properly distinguished from secular philosophy. Melanchthon argues that when the law is described as that which results in justification, Christianity and pagan philosophy are conflated. The law is accessible by means of natural revelation. This is why Melanchthon can praise Aristotle as an ethicist, while condemning the use of Aristotle as an expositor of Christian truth over and above the biblical text (Apol AC IV.16). He asks the question, "If this be Christian righteousness [philosophic righteousness], what difference is there between philosophy and the doctrine of Christ?" (Apol AC IV.12). Apparently some priests spent their time in the pulpit expounding upon the ethics of Aristotle while ignoring the biblical text. This demonstrates the concern for preaching in the writings of the early Reformers. Melanchthon certainly was not opposed to the exposition of morality from the pulpit, but he was concerned that, with an improper understanding of law and gospel, there would be no essential differentiation between Christian preaching and civic righteousness. There would then be nothing unique about preaching, and the message of the church would become, essentially, Christless.

In contradistinction to the Christless preaching of good deeds, a proper distinction between the law and the gospel allows one to confess the necessity of both faith and works within their proper contexts. That the balance between these two concepts is difficult is apparent in some of the controversies that arose in early Lutheranism. The Formula addresses two distinct errors in relation to these two realities of the Christian life. On the one hand, George Major argued that good works are necessary for salvation. This error is addressed in Article IV as a misunderstanding of the gospel. Though good works are an essential aspect of the life of faith, they are never saving; this is to confuse the proper spheres of the law and the gospel. Another writer, Nicolaus von Amsdorf, argued against the theology of Major by promoting the concept that good works are *injurious* to salvation. This also is a confusion of law and gospel, placing good deeds in a negative position when they are, indeed, commanded by God and necessary within their proper sphere. A proper understanding of both law and gospel, in their traditional formulations, guards against both legalism and antinomianism.

The concerns above demonstrate just a few of the most prominent practical concerns in expounding upon the distinction between law and gospel. Lutheran orthodoxy is not simply a collection of intellectualizing propositions, but has a concern for the teaching and practical ministry of the congregational pastor. This is nowhere more apparent than in the exposition of law and gospel. A correct understanding of this teaching aids the burdened conscience by granting assurance of forgiveness through the alien righteousness proclaimed in the gospel. Law and gospel also guards against antinomianism and helps the pastor to know when he is called to preach the law rather than the gospel so that one might not live in carnal security. Finally, a proper understanding of law and gospel aids the pastor in his ability to proclaim both faith and works, each within its proper sphere.

Conclusion

This chapter began with the question, *What are the scriptural and theological foundations for the distinction between law and gospel in confessional Lutheranism?* These theological foundations have been explored and outlined through a number of specific points. The law, in the Lutheran tradition, is defined as the eternal will of God. Though the term "law" is used in a broader sense at times, this narrower sense is the one utilized in reference to the law-gospel distinction. The term "gospel" similarly has a broader sense in which it refers to the entirety of Christ's teaching. It is, again, its narrow sense which is meant in this particular context. This narrow sense consists in the promises of God as founded in Christ. The law and the gospel share both differences and similarities. These two words of God differ in their impact upon the sinner. The law brings conviction and death; the gospel brings justification and life. These two teachings are *not*, however, contradictory. Though they produce opposite effects existentially, they are not set in contradistinction to one another ontologically. Both the law and the gospel are words of God, who is ontologically simple, and thus incapable of contradiction. Ultimately, there is unity between the law and the gospel within the content of the gospel itself. The gospel does not present grace that is devoid of justice; rather, by his passive and active obedience, Christ has fulfilled the divine law as a substitute and has vicariously paid the debt owed to God by sinful humanity. Furthermore, the law is itself good, not only in its connection with the gospel, but as a guide for God's creation. As God's eternal will, the law does not only provide a temporal function within this era of the church's existence. The law will remain eschatologically, though it will no longer need to coerce the believer into obedience, since the sinful flesh will be destroyed. In the present age, the law functions as both a guide for obedience and a tool of coercion toward the sinful flesh. It was demonstrated above that all of these considerations, in the confessional Lutheran tradition, are arrived at through careful exegesis, especially in passages found in Romans and Galatians regarding justification. These truths, furthermore, are all practical. This important and fundamental distinction between God's commands and promises is essential to daily Christian life, as well as to the work of the pastor and the local church.

The theological and scriptural foundations of the traditional confessional Lutheran law-gospel distinction have been explored. Now, for the purposes of this study, these theological truths will be contrasted over against contemporary perspectives on the law-gospel distinction, especially as expounded by Gerhard Forde and the Radical Lutheran school of thought. When examined together, it is demonstrated that there are areas of both continuity and discontinuity between these two theological traditions.

4

The Distinction between Law and Gospel in the Theology of Gerhard Forde Compared and Contrasted with Confessional Lutheranism

Introduction

IN THE PREVIOUS TWO chapters, the broader range of discussion surrounding the distinction between law and gospel and the traditional confessional Lutheran perspective on these issues have been exposed. In chapter two, the writings of Gerhard Forde were briefly examined in the midst of other relevant literature regarding this classic Lutheran distinction. In chapter three, the Lutheran confessional documents and classic Lutheran sources were explained in view of their perspective on law and gospel. In this chapter, the following question is answered: *How does the distinction between law and gospel as expounded by Gerhard Forde compare and contrast with that of confessional Lutheranism?* The doctrines explained in the previous two chapters in a variety of writers are compared to demonstrate that several similarities and divergences exist.

Both Gerhard Forde and the classical Lutheran theologians cited in the previous chapter claim to be inheritors of the Lutheran tradition. Furthermore, both argue, in opposition to one another, that they rightly explain Luther's own thought. Because of their common ancestors in Luther and other early Reformers, there are several areas of agreement between Forde and confessional Lutherans. Much of the terminology utilized by both is taken from the writings of Luther. Many of these terms, however, are explained in a different manner within these two divergent expositions of the Lutheran tradition. These similarities and differences will be explored topically, through an examination of Forde and the confessional Lutheran tradition on a variety of subjects. This begins with an expositions of the philosophical grounding of the theology of Gerhard Forde and of confessional Lutheranism. The differences in approach to metaphysics between these two traditions set the foundation for further disagreements on specific doctrines. This is followed by a discussion of the nature of the law, the atonement, the third use of the law, antinomianism, and sanctification. On each of these topics, there are areas of both continuity and discontinuity between Gerhard Forde and the Lutheran scholastics.

In this section, many of the resources cited in the previous chapters will be utilized. Forde's own thought will be explained through the two books examined above: *Where God Meets Man* and *The Law-Gospel Debate*. These two texts will be supplemented by various other writings of Gerhard Forde in which the issues in discussion are treated, including various essays and his contributions to the *Christian Dogmatics* series published by Fortress Press. For the confessional Lutheran position, the historic sources cited in the previous chapter will be used alongside contemporary resources explaining the Lutheran orthodox perspective on law and gospel.

Philosophical Foundations

While Forde never asserts a philosophical system, nor does he cite his philosophical influences, throughout his work it is apparent that he functions from some metaphysical convictions which underlie his thoughts. These philosophical underpinnings of Forde's theology differentiate his thought from that of confessional Lutheranism. Scholastic Lutheranism, though rejecting Greek philosophy in its magisterial use, functioned broadly under a classical substance metaphysic taken particularly from Aristotle. The broader philosophical assumptions of the Lutheran Reformers did not differ substantially from many others in the medieval church. Gerhard Forde, in contrast to this, writes in a post-Kantian context, therefore causing him to approach theology with varying views on reality—along with different terminology—than the Lutheran orthodox. This leads Forde to interpret the doctrines of law, gospel, atonement, God, and many other topics differently than earlier scholastic theologians. The philosophical background here will serve as a prolegomena of sorts to understand the rest of Forde's unique ideas in contrast with confessional Lutheranism.

Forde is a unique figure within Lutheran thought, and as such, there is no one particular influence upon his thought which overrides all others. He is not a heavily philosophical thinker, and does not often cite philosophers either ancient or modern. He does, however, draw heavily upon certain nineteenth-century theologians in his own research, and in doing so, has imbibed some of their unique ideas. In his doctoral dissertation, Forde outlines several figures whose thought influences his own on law and gospel and the Christian faith more broadly. Among these are J. C. K. von Hofmann, Theodosius Harnack, and Karl Barth. Another rather unknown influence on Forde is the early-twentieth-century Luther scholar Hans J. Iwand, whose work was not translated into English until 2008. The fact that these thinkers, among others, were influential upon the development of Forde's theology rather than the scholastics such as Chemnitz or Gerhard leads to some of the underlying philosophical convictions that distinguish him from confessional Lutheranism.

In *The Law-Gospel Debate*, Forde begins his discussion of the debates surrounding this subject with a controversy that arose between nineteenth-century orthodoxy and J. C. K. von Hofmann. While he does not affirm the entirety of Hofmann's own theological constructions, Forde praises his criticisms of the theology of Lutheran orthodoxy, including his rejection of scriptural inerrancy and vicarious satisfaction. Hofmann himself was a historicist, who attempted to locate Christian truth, and even the identity of God himself, within the process of historical development. Written in a nineteenth-century German theological context, Hofmann's ideas bear a striking resemblance to the growing idealism of his day, and to the figures Hegel and Schelling in particular. This is not to say that Hofmann himself simply echoes or Christianizes German idealism, as he is an original thinker in his own right. Matthew Becker notes that while Hofmann certainly drew upon and spoke the language of popular philosophers of his day, he ultimately viewed himself as a biblical rather than philosophical or speculative theologian.[1] While Forde does not adopt idealism in its entirety by any means, he acknowledges the usefulness of Hofmann's dismantling of the orthodox system. In particular, he praises Hofmann's rejection of the law as a set of eternal ideas, through his placement of the law as one particular era of redemptive history in a *Heilsgeschichte* schema. This criticism of Lutheran orthodoxy is not simply a statement about one particular locus of theology, namely the law, but of the fundamental orthodox tenet that

---

1. Becker, *Fundamental Theology*, 118–19.

being underlies the essence of reality rather than becoming. As an idealist, Hofmann views reality through the lens of historical process; as will be demonstrated, Forde similarly views reality through act rather than being, though in a personalized-eschatological sense.

Forde's approach to reality echoes thoughts of earlier figures such as Theodosius von Harnack and Karl Barth, though he himself differentiates his thought from these figures in numerous ways. Harnack, like Hofmann, draws heavily from the idealist tradition. However, Harnack was a harsh critic of Hofmann and other nineteenth-century theologians who argued that the dialectics of wrath and love could be overcome by some sort of synthesis, whether in the atonement or elsewhere. Forde praises his distinction between God "in Christ" and God "outside of Christ," which constitutes a "double relationship to the world."[2] Law and gospel both have their essence within the divine being and stand in contrast to one another with no simple solution. This leads to Forde's own dialectical approach to the faith which is mediated, in some sense, by neo-orthodoxy.

His rejection of a crucial distinction in Harnack's thought, however, demonstrates that Forde goes farther than Harnack in his rejection of traditional orthodox categories. While Harnack explains both law and gospel in terms of their effects upon the hearer, he distinguishes between the law's office and its essence. This preserves the essential nature of a law which has an existence that underlies its effect in history. While Chemnitz and Gerhard do not use this distinction explicitly, such a division is consistent with their exposition of the law. For Forde, such a distinction cannot exist. Instead, the law is defined by its office. This demonstrates Forde's fundamental conviction which underlies nearly all of his unique theological positions: being is defined by act. Everything is defined by what it does, rather than an essence that has independent existence behind that action. Forde praises Barth, who similarly rejects the *lex aeterna* as taught in Protestant scholasticism. It is Barth, in Forde's view, who first recognizes the eschatological nature of God's word of address to the individual. For Barth, God's word is such only as it directly addresses man. He differs from Forde, however, in his contention that this word is in a sense only *one* word, rather than the twofold word of law and gospel. Forde rejects Barth's approach to law and gospel, while simultaneously adopting his personalized-eschatological view of the word of God. For Forde, the word of God is not a set of propositions or specific

---

2. Forde, *Law-Gospel Debate*, 84.

words placed on a page; God's word is the dynamic action of law and gospel that impacts the hearer through Scripture and the sacraments.

These ideas, according to Jack Kilcrease, are largely Kantian.[3] While he is somewhat cautious in his association of Kant and Forde, Kilcrease notes that there seems to be a sort of noumenal/phenomenal divide in Forde's thought. Forde is always hesitant to speak of a thing-in-itself, relegating theological discussion to something's effects upon the human person. This is similar to the approach of neo-Kantians like Hermann Lotze, who influenced Abrecht Ritschl's interpretation of Luther. Kilcrease proposes that this may account for Forde's reticence to attach specific content to the law, speaking of the law instead as a dynamic force which brings about existential dread. Forde never utilizes this specific terminology, nor would he likely desire to do so. It is probable, however, that such a distinction (whether realized or not) comes through some of the neo-orthodox theologians who function with such presuppositions. If Kilcrease is correct in this matter, then Forde does in fact view the law as something which exists essentially apart from its effect upon the human person, though that essence remains inaccessible.

Rather than Kant, however, it is most accurate to say that it is existentialism which shapes Forde's thought more than any other philosophical movement. Without Kant, existentialism could likely not exist, and in that sense, Forde is influenced by Kant just as almost all twentieth-century and modern thinkers are (whether knowingly or not). It is beyond the scope of this study to examine the exact nature of the influence of Kierkegaard on Barth, the connection between Brunner and Buber, or of Heidegger's impact on Bultmann. However, in one way or another, it is indisputable that existentialist philosophy influenced the dialectical theology of the early through mid-twentieth century. Forde is a dialectical theologian. This is not to say that he is an overt Barthian, as he promotes a dialectical theological method of a somewhat different sort, but he shares many of the same concerns and presuppositions as Barth and others who are placed under the broad umbrella of "neo-orthodoxy." Like Barth, Forde seeks to emphasize the dynamic and personal nature of God's address through his word, while simultaneously rejecting the verbal inspiration theory of Protestant scholasticism. Like Barth, Forde rejects many of the philosophical presuppositions that underlie older Protestant thought in favor of a more dynamic view of reality.

3. Kilcrease, "Doctrine of the Law," 157.

Forde's approach to theology can accurately be labeled a personalized-eschatological approach. While Forde himself speaks broadly of "eschatology" as an underlying theme in his thought, such a term can be applied in numerous ways. A theology that is merely eschatological could be identified with a dispensational fundamentalist obsession with the relationship between the daily news and the Apocalypse of St. John. Theologians who are identified with the theology of hope surrounding Jürgen Moltmann, Wolfhart Pannenberg, and to a lesser extent, Carl Braaten, are certainly eschatologically minded, but not in the same personalized sense as is Forde. These writers view eschatology through the lens of a historical process of change in both the created realm and in God himself. Jenson, for example, proposes a doctrine of God which is thoroughly eschatological, wherein God is eternally future to himself through the person of the Holy Spirit.[4] For Forde, eschatology is not so much about historical process as it is about the individual's encounter with Christ in the gospel. Forde's eschatological emphasis is similar, though certainly not identical to, that of Rudolph Bultmann.

A brief examination of Bultmann's view of history will help to explicate some of the unique features of Forde's thought in relation to Lutheran orthodoxy. In his Gifford Lectures, published under the title *The Presence of Eternity: History and Eschatology*, Bultmann proposes his own view of what constitutes history from a Christian perspective. He rejects the idealistic view of history, which attempts to define history apart from man by a cosmic world process ever moving toward synthesis. Instead, Bultmann places history in man, and ultimately, in Christ. He identifies Christ as "*the eschatological event*,"[5] who is present through proclamation. Eschatology does not refer to a testable historical event, but to the act of God that takes place in preaching, in which the individual is set free in faith, and thereby becomes a new creation. Through faith, the Christian is both a historical being (in the sense of ordinary human history) and one who stands over and above history in the eschatological newness of Christ. He identifies this as Luther's *simul iustus et peccator*.[6] Forde, similarly, proposes that the eschatological event of faith arises through the proclamation of the gospel, which then places man in both this age and the age to come. Where Bultmann and Forde differ here relates to the nature of the human will in this eschatologi-

---

4. Jenson, *Systematic Theology* 1:207–23.
5. Bultmann, *Presence of Eternity*, 151.
6. Ibid., 154.

cal act. For Bultmann, man must continually make the decision for faith in response to God's action; for Forde, faith is unilaterally God's doing. The purpose of this comparison is not to assert that Forde agrees with Bultmann in every particular (he is no proponent of demythologization), but to demonstrate that his approach to the Christian faith, and eschatology in particular, can rightly be labeled "existential." Whether or not Heidegger had any direct influence on Forde, his ideas compare, in many ways, to that of the existentialist philosopher's students. To differentiate Forde's approach from that of other existentialist proponents of the Christian faith which is rather broad, the phrase used from this point forward to characterize Forde's approach to Christian theology is "personalized-eschatological."

This personalized-eschatological approach to theology and history differentiates itself from traditional Lutheranism through its neglect of a strong substance-metaphysic, and the general prioritization of act over being. While the Lutheran confessional documents do not themselves contain any kind of philosophical system, nor is there any conscious attempt to produce prolegomena, they do hold several statements which demonstrate the particular philosophical assumptions at work in the thought of the Reformers. These same assumptions are at work in the Lutheran scholastics as discussed in the previous chapter. The first point to be noted is simply that the Book of Concord includes the three ecumenical creeds, which function on the basis of classical metaphysics, and hence define God in terms of a specific essence who exists simultaneously in three persons. It is noteworthy that there was no attempt by the Lutheran Reformers to redefine classical theism in any substantial manner. Instead, the conclusions from the patristic and medieval era surrounding the doctrine of God are affirmed. This is especially clear in Article I of the Augsburg Confession, which presents a definition of God that includes his self-existence, and importantly, his simplicity. God is "without parts," meaning that he is not a composite being. For those who reject traditional Greek metaphysics, divine simplicity is often viewed as the most biblically unfounded and speculative of scholastic doctrines. The strong dialecticism in Forde negates the idea of some higher unity of law and gospel in God, and consequently, his simple essence. Yet, in the Augsburg Confession, the simplicity of God is strongly affirmed.

Perhaps most significant in terms of the philosophical assumptions inherent in the Lutheran Confessions is Article I of the Formula of Concord. This article is metaphysical in nature, as it surrounds a debate over the nature of the human essence according to the Lutheran theologian Matthias

Flacius. In his attempt to defend the pervasive nature of original sin, Flacius argued that sin is of the very essence of the human person, rather than an accidental category. Underlying this whole debate was the assumption that everything that exists has both an essence and accidental qualities. In their response to this controversy, the authors of the Formula of Concord do not reject or dismiss the Aristotelian categories used by Flacius and others involved in the debate. To the contrary, the Formula states that it is an "indisputable truth" that all things which exist are either a self-existing essence (*substantia*) or a non-essential quality which exists in something else (*accidens*) (FC SD I.57).[7] This might be described as a "static-ontological" concept of being. In contradistinction to Forde's contention, all things are defined (according to the Formula) by what they are *in essence*, not simply by their effects. This will all be expanded further as specific topics are addressed and compared.

Forde's personalized-eschatological approach to Christian theology and one that functions on the classical categories of substance and accident present alternative theological systems. If there is no thing-in-itself that the theologian has direct access to, but one instead must rely on existential encounter, one's approach to both law and gospel must fundamentally differ from classical Lutheranism. These differences are apparent in a variety of topics, but most foundationally, in the distinction between law and gospel.

Definition of the Law: Verba Dei and Opera Dei

The most fundamental differentiation between Forde's thought and that of confessional Lutheranism can be summarized by the distinction between the *verba Dei* and *opera Dei*. In their article "Why the Two Kinds of Righteousness?," Arand and Biermann, as previously exposed, differentiate between the law as God's work and as his word. When defined as God's word, the law is simply a reference to divine commandments, and the gospel to divine promises. This is definitional of what these words are. Chemnitz, Gerhard, and Pieper function with the same definition of law. The works of God are the *effects* of law and gospel respectively. In this sense, the law (in its second function) is identified with death, and the gospel with life. These realities are not what law and gospel *are* in essence, but what they *do* to the sinner. This echoes Harnack's earlier distinction between the essence of the law and the office of the law. For Forde, such a distinction does not exist,

---

7. These categories are consequently used in Lutheran scholasticism.

because there is no fundamental essence of an objective law which stands behind its impact upon the human creature.

According to Forde, the orthodox definition of the law, as exposited by Chemnitz and the following Lutheran tradition, is the very key to Protestant orthodoxy.[8] It is precisely this key which Forde purports must be discarded for a more dynamic and existential approach to the Christian faith broadly, and to law and gospel in particular. This "static-ontological" approach to the divine law informs the entirety of Lutheran orthodoxy, as Forde notes, including one's view of the gospel, Scripture, the atonement, and of God himself. Significantly, Forde does not cite any primary sources in his description of the Lutheran orthodox system in either his dissertation or other writings that exposit his criticisms of the theological school. The one orthodox theologian that Forde cites is E. W. Hengstenberg, who was a nineteenth-century German scholastic writer. Even in this case, Forde mostly cites secondary sources on this figure's theology. It appears that much of his information about Hengstenberg comes from the criticisms leveled against him by Hofmann. What is especially noteworthy about this is that Hengstenberg, while significant for a certain school of German theology in the nineteenth century, is not a dominant influence upon contemporary Lutheran orthodox writers. Lutheran orthodox theologians today are influenced more by seventeenth-century writers such as Johann Gerhard, Johannes Quenstedt, and Abraham Calov. A genuine and honest critique of Lutheran scholasticism would expose the teachings of these figures rather than one nineteenth-century theologian. While Forde does accurately describe Lutheran orthodoxy as proclaiming a view of the law as an eternal standard inherent in God's own nature, it is unclear whether he understands the existential and eschatological underpinnings of much earlier discussion surrounding law and gospel. The seventeenth-century orthodox theologians were not simply concerned with theology as a set of abstract concepts devoid of pastoral or practical implication. This is clear from the earlier sketch of confessional Lutheran perspectives on law and gospel, and is also addressed below.

Due to his lack of engagement with primary-source material, Forde's writing portrays a caricature of Lutheran orthodoxy. This is apparent in his explanation of the scholastic view of law and gospel as an "abstract and material distinction."[9] He argues that in orthodoxy, the law is simply

---

8. Forde, *Law-Gospel Debate*, 3.
9. Ibid., 7.

a set of propositions, and the gospel a set of different propositions. This supposed abstract approach is then distinguished from a "concrete" view of law and gospel wherein these ideas correspond to their effects upon human creatures.[10] Forde further argues that faith, in this schema, is defined as a cognitive acceptance of a series of propositions identified with the gospel. He connects this to the old scholastic approach to revelation, wherein Scripture is identified as the infallible word of God. With his general disdain for truth that is propositional and unchanging, Forde instead defines the word of God through its actions toward an individual rather than as an objective standard of truth. In his view, it is the scholastic perspective on the law which leads to its adherence to biblical infallibility. If the gospel is a set of propositions, the Bible must infallibly contain the propositions which are to be believed. This also promotes a static view of God who is bound to an objective set of laws which inhere in his own nature. Thus, the static-ontological concept of divine law limits the freedom of God. The caricatures made by Forde in this work deserve some interaction, as Lutheran orthodox works serve to correct such misunderstandings of the older theological system.

To be fair, Forde admits that his description of Lutheran orthodoxy could be dismissed as caricature, as he notes that there are further distinctions among the Lutheran orthodox which could temper some of the problems. He also points out that nineteenth-century orthodoxy is somewhat different from that of the seventeenth century.[11] Despite these important qualifications, Forde continues to contend that his basic overview of the scholastic tradition is correct. Again, there is certainly some truth to Forde's portrayal. These two traditions are, at heart, fundamentally opposed to one another. For Forde, the difference stems from their respective definitions of law. In his view, the orthodox understanding of a static law defines the entire theological system. While the interplay between various theological convictions is difficult to determine in terms of exactly what causes what, his portrayal does seem a bit simplistic. For Forde, the only reason why the Lutheran orthodox held to a strong view of inspiration, for example, is due to their convictions about the law. Beneath these disagreements is something much more fundamental: the relationship between act and being. For Lutheran orthodoxy, everything has a distinctive essence which can be defined as a thing-in-itself; for Forde, everything is defined by its dy-

10. Ibid.
11. Ibid., 9.

namic movement toward the human creature. For orthodoxy, law, gospel, atonement, Scripture, God, and so on are all defined by what they *are*. In Forde's theology, these are all defined by what they *do*. The place where this is most apparent is in their respective views of the law, but this fundamental presupposition, rather than simply the locus of the law, is the heart of this disagreement.

Regarding the locus of the law, there are some caricatures of Lutheran orthodoxy which must be addressed. First, it is simply not the case that Lutheran orthodoxy is concerned only with abstract propositional truth. Johann Gerhard, for example, was as much a devotional writer as he was a scholastic. Unlike some medieval scholastic writers, the orthodox Lutherans were always concerned to tie their discussions to practical realities in the lives of believers. Whether such a connection was always made with success is another question, but the principle behind their attempts stands. Like other doctrines, Lutheran orthodoxy addresses the law in its practical application to the sinner, instead of as just an abstract ideal in the mind of God. Gerhard makes such connections not only in his devotional writings, but throughout his *Theological Commonplaces*.

In the previous chapter, various writers from the Lutheran orthodox period and later orthodoxy were examined with a view to their understanding of law and gospel. In particular, the writings of Gerhard, Chemnitz, and Pieper were explained. Each author writes, primarily, about the law as it is contrasted with the gospel and its effects upon the human creature. This includes the law's bringing about a kind of existential dread. None of them view the law as a mere set of propositions. What Forde offers in this regard is a false dichotomy: either the law is a dynamic force in the life of the believer, or it is a mere set of static propositions. For orthodox Lutheranism, these have never been alternative perspectives, as both are necessary parts of the same reality. The law must first have a specific essence and content for its condemnatory value to have any coherence whatsoever. If such is not the case, what exactly is the law condemning one for? An eternal and concrete set of laws must exist for the law to have any condemning function at all.

Along with Forde's mischaracterization of the law in Lutheran orthodoxy, he also falsely accuses the scholastics of defining the gospel as a set of bare propositions. It is true, certainly, that there is propositional content behind the gospel. It is not simply an act of God devoid of any particular message whatsoever. One cannot escape the biblical reality that there is specific theological and historical content inherent within the gospel itself (1 Cor 15:1–8). This is not to say, however, that the gospel is *only* proposition. Like the law, the gospel has both an essence and a particular effect. As was explained in the previous chapter, in the Formula of Concord, Gerhard, Chemnitz, and Pieper all explain the gospel within the context of its contrast to the divine law, especially in relation to its saving activity. Similarly, faith is not explained as a cognitive acceptance of facts, but as a Spirit-given gift through which the Christian is united to Christ unto righteousness. Forde presents the common *notitia, assensus, fiducia* language as a pure intellectualizing of faith, as if the orthodox are attempting to exposit some kind of three-part process through which the believer jumps through the right intellectual hoops in order to receive salvation.[12] This, again, is a caricature of the orthodox, who did not describe these three ideas as "steps" to receive salvation, but as three aspects of the reality of God-given faith.[13] Such is especially clear in the contention that baptized infants receive faith. If the orthodox approach were a pure intellectualizing of faith, surely paedo-faith would remain an impossibility. The scholastics, in contrast to this characterization, argued that faith must not necessarily be reflexive, meaning that one might have direct faith in Christ without the intellectual ability to consider one's own faith.[14] Pieper, helpfully, writes that the following ideas are synonyms with faith in Lutheran orthodoxy:

> [D]esiring Christ (*velle*), seeking Christ (*quarere*), demanding Him (*expetere, desiderare*), as striving and running after Him (*in Christum tendere, in Christum ferri*), as stretching out the hands toward Him and embracing Him (*extendere manus, amplecti, complecti*), as coming to Him, approaching Him, running towards Him (*venire, accedere, currere*), as clinging to Christ and joining oneself to Him (*adhaerere Christo, se adiungere Christo*).[15]

Such ideas are a far cry from the contention that faith, for orthodoxy, remains some kind of intellectual assent to a variety of propositions. Forde does not read orthodoxy on its own terms and blatantly misrepresents its fundamental theological claims surrounding law and gospel.

Forde's description of law and gospel is by no means completely incongruous with Lutheran orthodoxy. In his emphasis upon the nature of the law as that which kills and the gospel as an instrument of life, Forde is

---

12. For a traditional Lutheran explanation, see Schmid, *Doctrinal Theology*, 410–11.
13. Pieper, *Christian Dogmatics* 2:430.
14. Schmid, *Doctrinal Theology*, 421.
15. Pieper, *Christian Dogmatics* 2:433–34.

perfectly consistent with the earlier Lutheran tradition. The problem, however, is that Forde has rejected the basic underlying content of both law and gospel in order to promote a so-called "dynamic" approach to the subject. In doing so, Forde has changed the very meaning of both terms by presenting his readers with an either-or scenario which is simply not necessary. One need not choose between the law as a dynamic force of God's wrath or as the eternal will of God. It is precisely *because* the law is God's eternal will that it takes on its dynamic character toward the sinner who violates it.

The Gospel and Atonement

Forde's incongruity with the traditional Lutheran understanding of law creates further division between his own thought and Protestant scholasticism in a number of areas. The first addressed here is the nature of the atonement, including both Christ's active and passive obedience. Since Forde purports that the static-ontological construction of the divine law impacts all areas of orthodox theology, he seeks to construct a different theology of atonement and justification which is consistent with his personalized-eschatological theology.

The basic argument behind Forde's rejection of the vicarious atonement as explained in seventeenth-century scholasticism is found in *Where God Meets Man*, as explained in the literature review above. While all of the material will not be repeated, an overview of certain aspects of Forde's argument is necessary for the present comparison. In this work, Forde speaks about a "ladder scheme" which makes up much contemporary Protestant theology.[16] This is essentially another manner in which he speaks about the static-ontological concept of divine law. It is supposed, according to Forde, that the law is like a ladder. In order for one to achieve salvation, one must climb this ladder in order to reach God, who remains at the top. In a Pelagian or other legalistic system, the sinner is to climb such a ladder with his own efforts. The Protestant orthodox, instead of rejecting the ladder scheme altogether, simply found another way to make such a concept work. It was proposed that the law still functioned as a ladder, but Jesus climbed this ladder as a substitute. This resulted in the creation of the categories of Christ's "active obedience" and his "passive obedience," through which Christ both obeyed the law on behalf of the human race and died a vicari-

---

16. This is alternatively called the "legal scheme" throughout Steven Paulson's *Lutheran Theology*.

ous death in place of sinners. According to Forde, such a theology does not actually solve the problem of the supposed "ladder scheme," but instead, seeks to explain it in another way. To truly present the eschatological newness of the gospel, one must reject the ladder scheme altogether, including ideas of Christ's substitutionary work.

Forde's personalized-eschatological presuppositions are at work here in a number of ways. First, Forde rejects any attempt to explain the atonement in any realm "out there" in the divine council, or as a transaction between God the Father and God the Son. In his view, this removes the atonement from the realm of concrete reality and places it into the theoretical. In metaphysical language, that approach to the atonement makes it about being, rather than a dynamic concrete act. Forde derides vicarious satisfaction as a simple "theory" about buying off God and removes its effectual nature.[17] He thus rejects the atonement model present in Pieper, Chemnitz, and Gerhard. Second, Forde repeats his criticism that faith cannot simply be an acceptance of objective facts, but arises through a divine encounter with God. He purports that if the gospel contains the specific doctrines about Christ's life and death as a substitutionary act, then it simply becomes another kind of law which one must accept in order to be saved.[18] Third, Forde argues that theology is not about propositions, but about God's "doing." He argues that theology which concerns itself with bare propositions, or with things as they are in their essence, is a theology of glory, or a theology "*about* the cross," rather than a theology *of* the cross.[19] Forde often uses language of the theology of glory in reference to a theology which concerns itself with the thing-in-itself, or in other words, those who concern themselves with a traditional substance-metaphysic, rather than with existential encounter. At one point, Forde is even bold enough to say that Christ "was not doing anything else in his death but dying."[20] Again, Forde is only concerned with the act itself, not with any objective being or content behind or informing that act.

These same ideas are present, in more detail, in Forde's essay "Caught in the Act," in which he explains his own ideas about the purpose and nature of the atonement. As is consistent with his actualized view of theology, he rejects the idea that any type of atonement theory can exist at all, and

17. Forde, *Where God Meets Man*, 11.
18. Ibid., 17.
19. Ibid., 33.
20. Ibid., 37.

that the act should not be approached "from above," in God's perspective, or in the realm of ideas.[21] With this in mind, Forde explains his rejection of various atonement theories. Not only does Forde reject vicarious satisfaction and other forms the Anselmian atonement model, but he also demonstrates flaws in the *Christus Victor* and subjective theories of the atonement as taught by Gustaf Aulen and several patristic writers. As much as these various models differ, they have a fundamental unity in their assertion that Christ's death has meaning in a logical scheme, in which there is some sort of obstacle for Christ to overcome. For Anselm, there is a need for God's honor to be satisfied, and thus Christ's death fits as the missing piece to this puzzle. *Christus Victor* similarly puts Christ's death in the realm of necessity in a scheme wherein the devil or demons need to be bought off by God. Even the exemplar theory, according to Forde, places a necessity on the atonement, as if Christ's love *must* be demonstrated through death on a cross. All of these ideas are false for one particular reason: they prioritize the ideas standing behind atonement rather than the act itself. Again, there is no access to any kind of "thing-in-itself" regarding the atonement, but only in terms of the realm of human experience.

To get rid of the supposed "theoretical" nature of other atonement models, Forde contends that an explanation of the atonement "from below" is the only proper way to approach the subject. Rather than any kind of necessity or ideas about *why* the cross happened, one must focus instead on the act itself. From this perspective, Forde argues that throughout his life, Christ offered unconditional forgiveness. He was not, as in Lutheran orthodoxy, actively obeying the divine law on behalf of sinful humanity; the purpose of his life was to offer and give forgiveness. Instead of receiving and accepting the forgiveness God offers in Christ, humans rejected this forgiveness. Human creatures do not want to be forgiven unconditionally, and for that reason, put Christ to death. In Forde's language, the death of Christ caught humanity "in the act."[22] The significance of the death of Christ, then, is that it reveals an evil act done by the entirety of humanity. It reveals how deeply God's creatures hate unconditional forgiveness.

There are some significant problems with such a perspective on the atonement. First, Forde assumes that it is indeed *all* of humanity that participated in the death of Christ and is guilty of putting him to death. There is, in his theology, no grounds or justification for making such a claim. If

---

21. Forde, *Preached God*, 90.
22. Ibid., 91.

one is to focus on the bare act itself, as an actual event apart from any metaphysical or theological system behind it, the reality is that only those Jews and Romans in the first century directly involved in the death of Christ are to be implicated. To argue otherwise is to make the atonement into part of a broader theological system, which Forde attempts to avoid. Viewed as a substitutionary sacrifice, it can properly be said that the death of Christ is an event which implicates all people, as his substitutionary work was done for the sins of all people. However, if no "transaction" like this was actually occurring, what is the relevant connection between a twenty-first century Christian and the death of Christ two thousand years prior? One is only left to speculate. Forde makes his claim with no attempt to demonstrate that such is the case either biblically or theologically.

The second problem with Forde's atonement theory is that he removes the cross from its position as a necessity. In his view, there is no *a priori* reason why the atonement must happen at all, as would be the case in all older atonement schemes, both objective and subjective. Since Forde rejects any discussion of the world of ideas and concepts behind the atonement, one can only attach a kind of *a posteriori* necessity of the atonement. There are two ways, then, in which Forde describes the atonement as an *a posteriori* "necessity" in some sense. First, it is a necessity from the human perspective. This is the only way in which sinners could possibly respond to a God who offers love and forgiveness unconditionally. Death is the only possible result of a confrontation between unconditional forgiveness and human creatures who do not want such forgiveness.

Second, in order for humanity to be saved, God must elect to be the God who is merciful, not a God of wrath. The atonement is the place in which God concretizes the essence of who he himself elects to be. In this way, the atonement results in a change within God's own being. Through the cross, the hidden God of wrath becomes the God of mercy. In Forde's words, God "becomes other" through his death.[23] Ultimately, it is the resurrection in which God is demonstrated to be the one who has elected to be merciful. This whole discussion is largely drawn from Barth's perspective on election and portrays a kind of actualism wherein God's own being is constituted by his free decisions in history, and especially on the cross.[24] While Forde consistently argues that God does not have to be reconciled to anyone (because the reality is that humans are reconciled, not God), he

23. Braaten, *Christian Dogmatics* 2:7.
24. Ibid., 69–76.

has not actually rejected what he sees as the fundamental problem of older objective atonement theories. For Forde, the atonement *is* about something which must happen to (or in) God. Rather than arguing that such a reality refers to a satisfaction of divine justice or honor, Forde contends that the change occurs in God's own being. In this sense, Forde has not actually escaped from the type of system he rejects. One might construct a possible "logical scheme" which stands behind the atonement in Forde's perspective. God is a God of wrath and a God of love. In order to save humanity, God must elect to be a God of love rather than a God of wrath. Thus, God chooses to become such a God through the cross of Christ. In this way, Forde has not escaped a logical atonement model at all. As much as he claims to proclaim an atonement model purely from "below," in which the death of Christ is *only* a death, he too seeks to give a kind of explanation to the cross. It simply is a different explanation than the older models. In fact, this actually makes the atonement *more* abstract than models of satisfaction. If the atonement is ultimately the place where God decides to be a God of mercy, the atonement itself simply becomes an outward demonstration of a reality which occurs in God's own being. In the Anselmian scheme, the historical event of Christ's death remains the place where redemption actually occurs. In Forde's perspective, redemption really occurs within God himself, and the cross is not necessary at all. It is a simple historical accident through which God's self-determination is manifest.

The third, and most significant, issue in Forde's theology of atonement is that he proposes that the cross is a solution to a human dilemma other than sin. For the Lutheran orthodox, sin is defined as a violation of divine precepts. Chemnitz and the following writers function with this concept of sin due to their convictions surrounding the law as God's eternal will. Through both original and actual sin, the human race incurs a debt, and thus places itself under God's wrath. The human problem is sin. The divine solution is forgiveness. While Forde often utilizes traditional language to describe sin and forgiveness, his fundamental redefinition of the law results in a redefinition of sin. Thus, while Forde might speak about redemption from sin, he utilizes such language in a way that differentiates him from confessional Lutheranism. This difference can be seen in the manner in which Forde speaks about God's wrath. Unlike some liberal theologians, Forde is adamant that God is indeed wrathful, and that such a topic is necessary to discuss. In orthodoxy, God's wrath is his anger toward that which offends his justice. Forde rejects this concept as part of the Anselmian atonement model. God, for Forde, is not bound by standards of justice; he is an absolutely free being. This is why God can forgive even without placating his justice through the cross. Forde equates God's wrath with his jealousy. Humanity is not under wrath due to its violation of the law, but due to its persistence in rejecting God's unconditional forgiveness and mercy. The question this raises is whether God's wrath has any objective existence at all. In Forde's thought, God has already determined to be the merciful God and *not* the God of wrath. This being the case, it appears that wrath can have no more logical existence within God, but merely within the experience of the human creature. This would imply universalism, though Forde refuses to endorse this idea as it is but another abstraction.[25] If wrath does exist in God, it exists merely as a kind of jealousy for those who refuse his grace. If wrath is not defined as God's anger toward, and hatred of, sin, can one really call it wrath at all? While Forde seeks to retain both wrath and grace in his theology in contrast to some strands of liberalism, he fails to uphold a doctrine of divine wrath in any traditional sense.

A second dilemma that Forde proposes is solved through the cross is the overcoming of the abstract and theoretical. One of the most prominent distinctions utilized in Forde's writing is that of the hidden and revealed God. The revealed God, for Forde, is the revelation of God in Christ proclaimed to the sinner. The hidden God is not only the God of wrath, but also the God of abstraction. He often identifies this with law, as well as the theology of glory. General truths and ideas are places where God is hidden. Forde distinguishes the mere "idea" that God has mercy from the actual concrete giving of mercy. Within the realm of ideas, even the concept of mercy is something from which people need to be saved.[26] God has, in general, always been merciful, but through the cross this mercy became particularized in the person of Christ. Thus, the atonement is the place where the realm of ideas is overcome, and love is brought to individuals through existential encounter with Christ. This further demonstrates Forde's continued prioritization of act over being. Divine love, in itself, has no effect when preached as a general concept, but is concretized through the "for you" proclamation of the gospel. While orthodox Lutheranism is certainly concerned with the actual giving of forgiveness through the means of grace rather than mere theorizing about the atonement, such a strict division between essence and act is not made. Lutheran scholastics devote extensive

---

25. Ibid., 93.
26. Forde, *More Radical Gospel*, 95.

space to descriptions of God's attributes, for example, which Forde would identify as the kind of abstraction that Christ redeems his people from.

When Forde states that the fundamental difference between himself and orthodox Lutheranism in terms of the definition of God's law has import for other areas of theology, he is correct. Through his rejection of the *lex aeterna*, Forde then redefines the gospel—most particularly, the atonement. Since the law is not an eternal standard of justice, Christ does not need to satisfy these standards through his life and death. This act is a historical accident through which all people are "caught in the act" and implicated for hating a God of mercy. Through being put to death, Christ then determines who God is to be—namely, a God of mercy rather than a God of wrath. This mercy is given through the proclamation of the gospel as a "for you" announcement, rather than stated as an abstract concept. The concepts of atonement found in Lutheran orthodoxy and in Forde are incompatible, and Forde's proposal fails at being a more convincing alternative to the traditional approach.

The Third Use of the Law and Antinomianism

One of the most prominent results of Forde's redefinition of God's law is his understanding, and ultimately denial of, the third use of the law. As Scott Murray catalogues, the rejection of the third use of the law is a common factor in twentieth-century Lutheranism. Writers such as Werner Elert and William Lazareth rejected the third use as an unfortunate move of Melanchthon following Luther's death. For Elert, the third use is a Calvinistic idea which some Lutherans just so happened to derive from Reformed theologians. Forde draws on many of these same criticisms in his denial of the law in its didactic function, but most importantly, his redefinition of law does not allow for a third use to exist. As has been demonstrated, Forde denies the distinction between the law's essence and office, restricting the law only to its *officium*—the condemnation of the sinner. Because the law takes on this negative form, there is simply no place for such existential despair to have any kind of positive function to guide one in obedience. If Forde were to acknowledge that the law has such a function, he could only do so by reverting to the Formula's own definition of the law as God's eternal moral will. Because he refuses to view the law in this manner, the nature of the Christian life, and sanctification in particular, differs from that of confessional Lutheranism in Forde's approach. This is demonstrated through an examination of Forde's perspective on the third use of the law, his writing on sanctification, and the two kinds of righteousness.

Foundational for Forde's rejection of the third use of the law is his personalized-eschatological approach to theology. Due to his strong dichotomy between this age and the age to come, Forde relegates the law entirely to the old age. It is not an eternal standard of moral living, but a necessary reality in a sinful age. The law, in a sense, *is* the old age, and the gospel *is* the new. Since Forde emphasizes discontinuity between these two ages, the law must be "emphatically and radically" excluded eschatologically.[27] Salvation is spoken of not simply as redemption from the curse of the law, but from the law itself. The law itself has been conquered in the Christ-event. The problem in utilizing such language is that the law, rather than sin, is spoken of as the human predicament. In traditional Lutheranism, the law, as God's eternal will, is a positive good. It only serves a negative function due to the presence of sin. While Forde is certainly not willing to disagree with Paul and declare that the law is not "holy, righteous, and good" (Rom 7:12), such appears to be the inevitable conclusion of such a schema.

One might get the impression from some of Forde's language that he is an antinomian. This is not true, at least in the fullest sense. The term "antinomian" itself has been utilized in a number of different ways throughout history, but it arose in a dispute between Luther and Agricola. Luther argued that Agricola was opposed to God's law because he argued that it should not be proclaimed in the church. It is only the gospel which the church proclaims; the law is for the courtroom. In a classical sense, then, the term "antinomian" refers only to those who reject the proclamation of the law altogether. In his essay "Fake Theology: Reflections on Antinomianism Past and Present,"[28] Forde addresses this issue and demonstrates that he is not, in fact, an antinomian. Instead, he argues that those who reject his personalized-eschatological understanding of the gospel are, in some sense, antinomians. This brief essay is helpful in expositing some of Forde's unique positions relating to God's law.

In this essay, Forde makes a distinction between two types of antinomianism Both of these perspectives, according to Forde, endanger the proclamation of the gospel and should be rejected. "Overt antinomianism" is the term used in reference to Agricola's theology. This perspective on the law is flawed due to its over-realized eschatology. Any attempt to banish

---

27. Forde, *Law-Gospel Debate*, 201.
28. As found in Forde, *The Preached God*.

the law altogether from the pulpit is a demonstration that one misunderstands the nature of the Christian's existence as *simul iustus et peccator*. Forde acknowledges, however, that the desire and goal of the antinomian is essentially correct. The law itself will come to an end, as the law is identified with sin and death, rather than an eternal order. He purports that Luther's statements in opposition to the first antinomians are not "pro-nomian," meaning that he does not argue from the perspective of the essential goodness of the divine law or promote the function of God's commands in a third use.[29] In this manner, Forde again differentiates himself from the Formula of Concord and the confessional Lutheran tradition. Chemnitz and Gerhard continually cite the goodness of the law as a reflection of God's eternal will in opposition to antinomianism. For Forde, such a perspective misses the nature of Christian eschatology.

The more common form of antinomianism, according to Forde, is "covert antinomianism." He identifies this covert antinomianism with those who seek to change either the nature or function of the law, rather than simply dismissing the law altogether. Forde's two primary targets are liberals who seek to explain their way around various moral laws in an attempt to soften or change God's demands, and the Lutheran orthodox who purport that there is a third function of God's law which remains for the Christian. According to Forde, both perspectives fail to comprehend the eschatological newness of the gospel and attempt to force the law into the new age. A favorite analogy of Forde is that any attempt to put the law into the new age is to put new wine into old wineskins. When this occurs, Forde argues that the only purpose of the gospel is to make room for a further use of the law. This is supposedly due to the fact that people have a "nervousness about the effectiveness of the gospel."[30] The only manner in which one can avoid such "covert antinomianism" is to adopt Forde's personalized-eschatological view of the Christian faith.

There are some significant problems with Forde's refutation of the supposed error of "covert antinomianism." First, Forde uses the term "antinomianism" in a sense which is incommensurate with its use in the rest of Christian history. In order to avoid the charge of antinomianism himself, Forde seems to redefine the term around his own theology so that it is not he, but everyone else, who is some sort of antinomian. The result of this is that not just orthodox Lutheran, but traditional Christian theology is

29. Forde, *Preached God*, 218.
30. Ibid., 220.

painted as "antinomian." This label is applied to all who have utilized the distinction between the moral, civil, and ceremonial laws.[31] The threefold distinction has its roots in the writings of Irenaeus and was standardized in the Western church through the writings of Thomas Aquinas. Such a threefold division was adopted by Protestants, both Lutheran and Reformed, as well as in Roman Catholic theology. Thus, the majority of Western theology is implicated in Forde's critique. For such a broad claim as Forde makes, he fails to substantiate his use of the term "antinomian" in reference to such a theology.

The second issue is that there indeed have been historical definitions of antinomianism which do in fact refer to some of the same propositions made in Forde's writings. The first confessional document of any Christian tradition to condemn antinomianism is the Formula of Concord, which rejects both the denial of the law's function in the church altogether (as in Agricola's thought) *and* a simple denial of the law's third use. Furthermore, the term "antinomian" has been used at times in reference not only to those who deny any function of the law from the pulpit whatsoever, but also to those who reject its third use. Kolb, Arand, and Wengert note that this term was utilized in the sixteenth century in connection with Musculus, who denied the third function of the law.[32] Similarly, in seventeenth-century English theology, there were a number of theologians who sought to downplay the positive function of the law to the point of rejecting the third use altogether. This resulted in the descriptor "antinomian" in reference to such figures as Tobias Crisp and John Eaton. While this debate occurred among Puritans rather than Lutherans, it does demonstrate further that there has been a broader application of the term "antinomian" than merely in reference to the form of theology taught by Agricola. No one prior to Forde, however, has used this term in reference to those who *affirm* the third use of the law. The accusation leveled by Forde here is unwarranted and has no historical precedent whatsoever.

It is not unwarranted to say then that Forde is an antinomian *of sorts*. This is not to say that Forde has no concern for ethics or that he denies that the law's functions in the life of the believer. He does, however, deny that the law has a positive function for the Christian and at times makes an exact identification of the law with sin and death. In this way, it might be said that Forde himself is a "covert antinomian," as much as he states

31. Ibid., 220.
32. Kolb, *History and Theology*, 199.

otherwise. It is also noteworthy here that even when speaking of the law in its second, or pedagogical, function, Forde does not utilize this aspect of the law in the same manner as the confessional Lutheran tradition. Because the law, in confessional Lutheranism, is a reference to God's eternal will, the second function of the law refers to the work of God through his commandments whereby he shows the sinner's shortcomings and sins. For Forde, the law is an existential encounter and is therefore not tied to specific commandments.

For this reason, Forde often identifies the gospel itself with the second function of the law. He notes that when "God imputes righteousness he makes us sinners at the same time."[33] Throughout his writings, and especially in his book *Justification by Faith: A Matter of Life and Death*, Forde argues that sinners understand themselves to be such *not* by the preaching of the law, but through the gospel. Sinners do not first see their sinfulness through the proclamation of God's moral imperatives and then look to the forgiveness of sins found in the gospel. Instead, the individual hears God's word of unconditional forgiveness, and then consequently reasons that if such forgiveness was given, then sin must have preceded it. In this manner, Forde agrees with Krister Stendahl's criticism of Luther's reading of Paul in essentially stating that "solution precedes plight."[34] This is why Forde often speaks about the cross of Christ, rather than the commandments themselves, as the greatest proclamation of law. If law is only an existential encounter which does the act of bringing one to despair, it can be attached to nearly anything, including the gospel itself. Thus, while Forde continues to uphold the necessity of the law in Christian proclamation, he does not speak of it in terms of specific moral imperatives. This is reflected in his own sermons, in which the exposition of divine commandments is not commonplace. For those who adopt a traditional Lutheran perspective on God's law, this can be labeled a moderated form of antinomianism.

There is a broad divergence between Gerhard Forde and the confessional Lutheran tradition surrounding the third use of God's law. The difference is not simply that Forde affirms what the scholastic Lutheran theologians teach regarding the first two uses of the law and only rejects the third. The difference between these two traditions runs much deeper and surrounds the nature and essence of the law. Forde's rejection of the third use of the law stems from two primary convictions. First is his

33. Forde, *Justification by Faith*, 31.
34. Stendahl, *Final Account*, 9-20.

personalized-eschatological view of the Christian faith. Because of the strict dichotomy between the two ages, the law and gospel are identified with the old and new age, respectively. Thus, eschatology supersedes the law. Second, Forde's definition of the law which identifies it as such only in the context of its effect negates any need for a positive function of the law. Confessional Lutherans believe in the third use of the law because the law is a reflection of God's eternal will. Without this underlying conviction, the third use no longer makes sense. These differences surrounding the third use of the law also point to differences in terms of the second use of God's law between the two traditions. For traditional Lutheranism, the second function of the law is tied to specific commandments; for Forde, it has no particular correlation to divine commands, and the gospel itself often functions as law. These difference are further explicated through an evaluation of how these two traditions speak about the nature of sanctification and the two kinds of righteousness.

Sanctification

One's view of the third use of the law has profound implications for the doctrine of sanctification. As with other doctrines, there is a large divergence in understanding regarding sanctification between Forde and the confessional Lutheran tradition. In classical Lutheranism, a distinction is made between justification and sanctification. The first term refers to one's state before God, whereas the second references an internal change whereby one is gradually conformed to the image of Christ. Sanctification is demonstrated through one's obedience to God's law as a reflection of his eternal will. Since Forde rejects the law in its third use, his perspective on sanctification and the Christian life differs from that of earlier Lutheran theologians.[35]

Forde has addressed the issue of sanctification in both scholarly and popular writings, and throughout his career his basic arguments surrounding this doctrine remain the same. His fundamental contention surrounding the life of sanctification is that this term refers not to a gradual growth in obedience to God's law (as orthodox Lutheranism teaches) but as a process of coming to a greater existential understanding of justification. In his discussion of this topic in his essay "The Christian Life" in Braaten and Jenson's *Christian Dogmatics*, Forde presents his view in opposition to

35. I have written on the topic of sanctification in Cooper, *Hands of Faith*.

the Lutheran scholastic tradition. He purports that there is a broad chasm between the perspective of Luther and that of the second generation of Lutheran theologians. In Luther, justification brings about an end to the law, and the law then has no relevance to sanctification whatsoever. The gospel is God's *final* word to the sinner, after which no word of law can or should be added. For the scholastics, the eschatological nature of justification is neglected, and the law is viewed as an ongoing rule for the Christian following justification. Forde uses a phrase from Luther to argue that the Protestant scholastics formed an approach to sanctification "after the fashion of Aristotle."[36] This is blamed on the static-ontological concept of God's law adopted by the Formula of Concord, which according to Forde displaces the centrality of justification.

In his rejection of the Lutheran orthodox perspective on sanctification, Forde also rejects a purely forensic understanding of *justification*. In his view, the great divide between justification and sanctification that occurred in the later sixteenth century was an unfortunate development. Along with causing an Aristotelian view of sanctification to predominate, this also caused Lutherans to ignore the dynamic eschatological approach to justification found in Luther. This, again, is based upon one's understanding of the law. For the orthodox, the law is God's unchangeable standard which must be obeyed. Christ obeys as a substitute through both his active and passive obedience. Justification is, then, the application of this work whereby Christ's merit, including his law-keeping and his substitutionary death, is applied to the one who has faith. Since Forde rejects these fundamental convictions which underlie the scholastics' understanding of the law, he consequently denies their forensic notion of justification. For Forde, the proper context in which one should speak of justification is as a metaphor of death and life. The law brings death, and the gospel brings life.

Personalized eschatology is, again, at the heart of Forde's conviction surrounding this matter. Justification is not defined by the transfer of any objective content or data from one party to another. To speak in this way would promote a non-dynamic approach to salvation, wherein salvation is achieved by some kind of "essence" of righteousness, rather than a divine encounter. For Forde, again, justification is defined by the existential act of the believer dying and rising in faith, and *not* by something objective in the heavenly courts. Because of this, Forde rejects the formulation of an *ordo salutis*. By adopting a purely forensic understanding of justification,

36. Braaten, *Christian Dogmatics* 2:426.

Lutheran orthodoxy had to somehow explain the connection between the purely forensic act of justification and the believer's works in this world. The objective-subjective dichotomy was thus overcome through the creation of an *ordo salutis*, which Forde argues includes a number of steps which the believer must walk in order to receive salvation. If, in the *ordo salutis*, justification precedes sanctification, Forde argues that sanctification necessarily becomes the central reality and justification recedes into the background.

Before proceeding to expand upon some of the specifics of Forde's perspectives on sanctification, his criticisms of Lutheran orthodoxy regarding the relationship between justification and sanctification merit a response. The first point to be made in response to his characterization of a supposed displacement of justification is that for the Lutheran orthodox, justification is never an isolated event from sanctification. Forde criticizes the separation of forensic justification and any inward change as a mere "effect" of justification. Contrary to Forde's contention, however, it is precisely the language of "effect" that keeps justification a central reality in Lutheran thought. In the Reformed theological tradition, there is an extensive amount of debate surrounding the exact nature of the relationship between justification and sanctification. Michael Horton and a few others have argued that justification is in some sense a cause of sanctification. Many others have opposed this, and have argued instead that there is no intrinsic connection between justification and sanctification. Richard Gaffin argues that the central soteriological category in Pauline thought is union with Christ.[37] Through faith, one is united to Christ and receives the twin benefits of justification and sanctification. Justification is not a cause of sanctification, and they have no inherent connection to one another. In this type of system, it is clear how justification can be removed from its central position in the *ordo salutis*. For the Reformed writer, sanctification can be spoken of without any mention of justification at all, since no causal relationship exists. For the Lutheran orthodox, however, it is precisely *because* sanctification is an effect of justification that the doctrine of sanctification can never be isolated. Justification continues to be the fuel for sanctification, and a consistent Lutheran *ordo salutis* will never relegate justification to the background.

The second point to be made in response to Forde's criticism is that he supposes the Lutheran orthodox view to speak of justification as a mere past event in the *ordo salutis*. This is reflective more of a Calvinistic approach to the order of salvation than the one found in Lutheran scholasticism. Two

---

37. Gaffin treats this in his volume on the Pauline *ordo salutis*, *By Faith, Not by Sight*.

American Lutheran theologians who are heavily scholastic in both writing style and influence, Adolf Hoenecke and Revere Franklin Weidner, mention that the act of justification is continuous.[38] God does not simply declare the believer righteous at the moment of initial faith only to then get the believer to work at the "real business" of sanctification. At every instant, God is continually declaring the believer to be righteous for the sake of Christ. This is reflected in the citation of Gen 15:6 in Rom 4. Paul cites Abraham as an example of the justification of the ungodly (Rom 4:5) not simply at the beginning of his life of faith, but after he had been living in faithfulness for many years. Like Abraham, the believer continually lives in God's justification. If it is understood that justification is a daily reality, there is then no reason why it would be neglected or replaced by a doctrine of sanctification.

The two-kinds-of-righteousness paradigm demonstrates further why Forde's argument surrounding the displacement of justification in confessional Lutheranism is mistaken. According to Arand and Biermann, the two kinds of righteousness—namely, active and passive—define the nature of the human creature's two essential relationships.[39] Active righteousness is that which guides the believer in relation to other human persons. In this realm (*coram mundo*), the law, rather than the gospel, functions as the determinative factor in these relationships. God has given his creatures laws as standards which he desires for them to follow. This earth, then, is the realm of sanctification. It is love, rather than faith, which serves the neighbor in need. The divine-human relationship functions differently, however. This relationship is established and maintained solely by faith. The law does not constitute or maintain this relationship. Within this framework, Forde is correct that the reality of justification truly is the "end of the law." In a *coram Deo* context, there is no law after the gospel. Justification is God's final and ultimate word to the sinner. Sanctification does not somehow displace justification as determinative of one's relationship to God. In this way, Forde's criticisms of both progressive sanctification as an event of the *ordo salutis* which follows justification, and of the third use of the law, are mitigated, while his concern to keep justification the central reality of the Christian life is affirmed. As long as one continues to live in relation to God, justification remains the central reality of Christian faith and life.

---

38. Hoenecke, *Evangelical Lutheran Dogmatics* 3:175. Weidner, *Pneumatology*, 167.
39. Arand, "Why the Two Kinds."

Thus far, Forde's criticisms of the traditional approach to Christian obedience have been explained. He does not, however, only seek to criticize the earlier tradition but also formulates his own perspective on what constitutes Christian sanctification. In what is perhaps his most well-known writing, an essay titled "The Lutheran View of Sanctification," Forde expounds upon his perspective on the subject in contrast to other popular perspectives in the broader Christian world. In this article, he proposes that sanctification is defined as "the art of getting used to justification."[40] There is no sharp line of division between justification and sanctification, and thus sanctification simply becomes the existential self-understanding that one is justified solely by faith. The old creature within each person continues to desire self-justification, and thus must be continually reminded that justification occurs by faith. This work is *not* to be identified with the moral life. In Forde's view, Luther did not strongly differentiate between the believer and unbeliever in terms of moral living. While the Lutheran orthodox utilize the term "civil righteousness" to speak about the works of the unbeliever, Forde argues that the term should be used to speak about Christian obedience.[41] Such moral or virtuous living is a product of the old age rather than the new. The only aspect of Christian living that can be positively identified with sanctification is that which is completely free, un-coerced, and even "God's secret," unknown to the individual performing the deeds.[42] These various distinctive positions of Forde on this issue are attempts to unify justification and sanctification in one concrete reality.

In identifying justification and sanctification, Forde is not completely discordant with Lutheran orthodoxy. He notes, for example, that the term "sanctification" is often used in Scripture as a synonym for justification, as in 1 Cor 1:2, for example.[43] This fact is recognized by the Lutheran orthodox, which is why a division is made between two uses of the term "sanctification." In its broad sense, sanctification is a reference to the entire act of salvation, with a particular emphasis on justification. In this way, one can speak of a past tense in sanctification, wherein one is presently and perfectly holy on account of Christ. Along with this, there is a narrow sense of the term which refers to one's ongoing progress into a life of holiness. Forde essentially rejects any use of sanctification in the narrow sense and

---

40. Forde, *Radical Gospel*, 226.
41. Ibid., 227.
42. Ibid.
43. Ibid., 229.

prefers to use the broad sense exclusively. In his view, the only reason why people began distinguishing between justification and sanctification in the post-Reformation era was a fear of preaching unconditional grace.[44] Such a motivation is impossible to substantiate, but it must be pointed out that the entire Lutheran scholastic tradition bases its discussion of the narrow sense of sanctification not on some fear that justification should be tempered by something else, but on a variety of scriptural texts which clearly speak about progress in the moral life of believers.

A significant problem in Forde's approach to sanctification is his lack of exegetical argumentation. In Lutheran orthodoxy, the discussion of sanctification is based on an in-depth theological treatment of a variety of biblical texts, but Forde mostly discusses one's existential Christian experience. This is not to say that he does not employ Scripture *at all* in these discussions, as he correctly notes that there are places in the New Testament wherein the language of sanctification is used in a positional, rather than progressive, sense. He also is fond of utilizing Rom 6 in his exposition of sanctification, which he argues should remain the central Pauline text in this discussion. However, Forde simply does not treat various other texts in which the doctrine of progressive sanctification has been taken up by orthodox theologians. If the scholastics were wrong about the nature of sanctification in its narrow sense, such must be demonstrated by a thorough refutation of their various biblical arguments rather than a simple dismissal of their proposals. At one point, Forde even acknowledges that one will raise the objection that Paul's Epistles follow gospel indicative with imperative statements about how believers are to live. However, rather than explaining how these texts fit into his proposal about sanctification, he dismisses such an objection as an attempt to put conditionality on the gospel promise.[45] Without a thorough exegetical treatment of the nature of sanctification and good works in the New Testament, Forde's view of sanctification as the process of gaining a greater existential self-understanding of justification remains unconvincing.

As in other areas of theology examined previously, Forde is not in complete disagreement with Lutheran scholastic thought surrounding the nature of sanctification. Both traditions affirm that it is the doctrine of justification, rather than sanctification, that is at the center of Christian faith and life. The exposition of this idea, however, differs between the two

44. Ibid., 230.
45. Ibid., 232.

traditions. For Forde, justification can only remain central if one rejects the notion of progressive sanctification. For the confessional Lutheran tradition, especially as developed in view of the two kinds of righteousness, there are two ways in which justification can remain the central reality of the Christian life without neglecting progressive sanctification. First, justification can be spoken of as a continuous forensic declaration rather than a past event which simply begins the Christian life. Second, the distinction between one's life *coram Deo* and *coram mundo* allows one to retain the centrality of divine imputation in one sphere while acknowledging the reality of sanctification in the other. There is therefore agreement between Gerhard Forde and confessional Lutheranism that the gospel is God's final word *coram Deo*. For the scholastics, however, it is *not* God's final word with regard to one's place in creation. While Forde addresses genuine practical and pastoral concerns in his development of sanctification, these same concerns are already addressed in the traditional Lutheran scheme in a manner which is more consistent with the biblical text.

Conclusion

In this chapter, the similarities and differences between Gerhard Forde and confessional Lutheranism have been explored. There are some significant areas of agreement between these two interpretations of the Lutheran tradition. Both have a concern to explain the effects of law and gospel upon the individual, which correspond to death and life respectively. Similarly, both contend that the death of Christ is the place in which redemption occurs, and that the atonement is not a mere moral example, but a saving event. Finally, both Forde and confessional Lutheranism seek to retain justification by faith as the central reality of the Christian life and build a doctrine of sanctification which is intimately related to justification. Despite these significant areas of agreement, however, the two approaches to the Lutheran faith have vastly divergent approaches to Christian faith and life.

The most foundational disagreement between the scholastic Lutheran writers and Gerhard Forde is the underlying philosophy which grounds their respective systems. The Lutheran orthodox writers were committed to an essentialist metaphysic, wherein each thing has an essence which is distinguished from its actions. Forde, in contrast to this, conflates act and being. This difference is most clearly expressed with their respective understandings of God's law. For the orthodox, the law's office and essence are differentiated from one another. The law, in *essence*, is the eternal will of God, and its *office* in a fallen world is the accusation of sinners. Forde rejects such a distinction and defines the law itself by its act upon the individual. These incommensurate views on the law lead to two differing perspectives on the atonement. For orthodoxy, the atonement is a vicarious sacrifice by which Christ passively takes the penalty due to lawbreakers upon himself in the place of sinful humanity. Since Forde rejects the "static-ontological" concept of the law, he reformulates the atonement as an action "from below," which ultimately is the place wherein God elects to be a God of mercy rather than a God of wrath. The two divergent views on God's law lead to two different accounts of the gospel.

Further, the Christian life is explained in a different manner in Forde's writings than in confessional Lutheranism. For the scholastics, God's law—as the immutable will of God—has three distinctive functions: to curb sin, to demonstrate one's sinfulness, and to guide the believer's decisions and actions. Since the law, for Forde, is not an objective set of propositional commandments, there is no place for a third use of the law at all. Instead, the law is defined only by its second function, though Forde does acknowledge the validity of the civil use of the law. This is further explained through Forde's personalized-eschatological approach to theology, wherein the law is only a product of the old age and will ultimately be superseded at the Parousia. For orthodoxy, the law reflects God's nature and thus will never pass away. Forde's rejection of the law's third function also informs his unique approach to sanctification. For the orthodox, justification and sanctification are two discrete elements of the *ordo salutis*, with justification being the cause of sanctification. Forde argues against this objective-subjective distinction with the concern that the traditional approach displaces justification from its central position. Furthermore, since Forde rejects the third use of the law, he denies that sanctification consists in a gradual increase in obedience to God's commandments. Instead, for Forde, sanctification is defined as coming to a greater understanding of justification. All of these differences will be explored in view of their practical and pastoral implications in the following chapter, which addresses the question, *What are the implications of the dissonance between Gerhard Forde and confessional Lutheranism?*

5

Conclusion

Implications of the Dissonance between Gerhard Forde and Confessional Lutheranism

Introduction

IN THE PREVIOUS CHAPTERS, the perspectives of Gerhard Forde and confessional Lutheranism on the topic of law and gospel have been examined and evaluated. It has been demonstrated that these two interpretations of Lutheranism are inconsistent with one another and present two alternative theological systems. The question answered in this chapter is, *What are the implications of the dissonance between Gerhard Forde and confessional Lutheranism?* In the previous chapters, the specific doctrinal content of such disagreement has been discussed, but the present chapter is more practical in nature, as these disagreements are explained in terms of practical and pastoral theology which impact the church at large.

The method of treatment in this section is to first explicate the conclusions reached thus far in this study. Following these conclusions, practical implications will be explored. First, let us deal with the nature of preaching in these two divergent approaches to the Lutheran faith. Again, while similarities exist between these streams of thought due to their common Lutheran heritage, there are significant implications for the act of preaching within each system. Preaching will be explored in light of the definition of the law as either an existential encounter between God and the sinner, as in Forde's thought, or as the eternal will of God, as in Lutheran scholasticism. These present alternative methods of preaching law, gospel, the atonement, and sanctification. Second, the question of ethical formation will be

Conclusion

explored between these two different traditions, and the application of the Christian faith to daily ethical choices will be exposited. Third, the areas of further exploration on this topic will be explained, as further research should be done in the future upon the issue addressed in this work. Finally, a conclusion is included which summarizes the findings of this project throughout.

Major Insights Gleaned from This Study

Up to this point, several conclusions can be drawn in relation to the contrast between Gerhard Forde and the confessional Lutheran tradition. These conclusions are presented here so that the practical implications of these differences can be explicated in light of these previously explored topics. While Forde and historic Lutheranism share several similarities in their respective approaches to law and gospel, the differences are vast and impact a significant number of doctrinal topics.

This study began by asking the question, *In what ways are Gerhard Forde's views concerning the distinction between law and gospel dissonant from what is affirmed in confessional Lutheranism?* This question has been addressed throughout the study, as various elements of Forde's views have been demonstrated to be incompatible with confessional Lutheranism. This was then followed by the question, *What is the current state of scholarship concerning the distinction between law and gospel made within the Lutheran ecclesial tradition, including that articulated by Gerhard Forde?* The proposals of Forde, Scaer, Kilcrease, Murray, Arand, and Biermann were presented and evaluated so that the general landscape of theological scholarship on this issue was set forth. Following this question, I asked, *What are the scriptural and theological foundations for the distinction between law and gospel affirmed in confessional Lutheranism?* These foundations were laid through an examination of the Lutheran Confessions, the works of Martin Chemnitz, and the writing of Johann Gerhard. Following this, the next question asked was, *In what ways does the distinction between law and gospel articulated by Gerhard Forde compare to and contrast with the confessional Lutheran understanding?* It was shown that though there are areas of agreement, these two traditions are generally inconsistent with one another. In this final chapter, in light of the previous conclusions, the concluding question is asked: *What are the implications for confessional Lutheranism of recognizing the dissonant views espoused by Gerhard Forde regarding the distinction between law and gospel?*

The primary differentiating factor between Gerhard Forde and confessional Lutheranism is their different underlying metaphysical convictions. While the Lutheran scholastics generally adopt a traditional Greek metaphysic, with the conviction that everything has a unique essence which stands behind its actions, Forde argues that theology should not be defined in static terms, but by its act upon the human subject. Another way of explaining this difference is to say that for Forde, there is no "thing-in-itself" that the human subject has any direct access to, and thus the theologian is not concerned with such ideas. This leads to two different approaches to both the law and the gospel. For Forde, the law is not defined by what it is, but instead by what it does to the sinner. There is no distinction between the law's office and its essence, but it is defined solely in terms of its office (in a second-use sense). For Chemnitz, Gerhard, and the Formula of Concord, the law is the eternal will of God, and its essence stands apart from its accusatory function. The law, for the scholastics, is eternal in nature, whereas Forde views it as temporal. The confessional approach to the law is derided by Forde as a "static-ontological" concept of God's commands. For Forde, the law does not have any direct connection to commands as such—instead, whatever accuses is law. This results in a rejection of the third function of the law. The Formula of Concord explains the law in terms of a threefold use, which includes a civil, an accusatory, and a didactic sense. This threefold division is maintained by the following Lutheran traditions, and contemporary confessional Lutheran writers such as David Scaer and Scott Murray defend the third function of God's commands as a positive good in the life of the believer.

These differences surrounding the law lead to a different approach to the gospel. For Lutheran scholasticism, there is an intimate connection between the law and the gospel. While these two concepts are contrasted in terms of their impact upon sinners, they are not contradictory in essence. The gospel comprises Christ's active obedience, which refers to his fulfillment of the law, and his passive obedience, or his suffering the penalty of law-breaking on behalf of sinful humanity. In this way, the law itself is fulfilled as an aspect of the gospel. For Forde, the law has no role in salvation in any sense. This doctrine concerning Christ's fulfillment of the law, in Forde's view, is part of the "ladder scheme," which teaches that the law is something that must be obeyed in order for one to achieve redemption. For

Conclusion

Forde, it is irrelevant whether it is the human subject or Christ himself who must fulfill the law; either way, the law is mistakenly placed in the category of redemption. For Forde, the gospel is radically separated from the law. He proposes a personalistic-eschatological approach to the gospel, wherein the law belongs to the old age and the gospel to the new. One exists under both only insofar as the believer is in the tension between being a historical creature bound by law and an eschatological being set free through the gospel. At the Parousia, such a tension will no longer exist, and the law will cease altogether.

There are several other implications of Forde's system which differentiate it from classical Lutheran thought. The doctrine of God is profoundly impacted through Forde's redefinition of law. In the scholastic tradition, the general tenets of a Thomistic view of divinity are affirmed, such as God's immutability, consistency, and simplicity. Forde prefers not to utilize such static categories, but instead defines God himself in terms of his act in Christ. This is especially clear in his view of the cross, wherein God's own being is constituted by his decision to be a God of grace through the atonement. The manner in which Forde describes the law and the gospel also promotes a God who contradicts himself with these two words. The confessional Lutheran tradition contends that, though mystery exists in terms of the relationship between God's love and wrath, these elements of the divine being are not essentially inconsistent with one another.

On a purely theoretical level, the distinctions between Forde and the Lutheran confessional tradition are immense. Each locus of the theological system is affected by Forde's redefinition of the law and his consequent revision of the gospel. These differences are far from merely academic, however, as one's perspective on law and gospel determines the nature of practical and pastoral ministry. Below, these practical and pastoral implications are explored in light of the differences expounded throughout.

Preaching and Forde's Theological System

Like any theological movement, Forde's view of Christian doctrine has a profound impact upon what is spoken from the pulpit. His perspective on the law, gospel, atonement, sanctification, and ethics leads to a unique view of proclamation at the center of the pastoral ministry. Here, Forde's view is examined and critiqued as inconsistent with a confessional approach. Throughout this discussion, three particular works are utilized to exposit

Forde's theology of preaching and the broader effect of these views upon the Lutheran world. First is Forde's book *Theology Is for Proclamation*, which is a theological prolegomena of sorts, through which he characterizes the theologian's task as one of proclamation. This volume identifies several of the key elements of Forde's thought and applies them to the act of preaching. Therefore, this work is the most essential one in a determination of the influence that his theology has upon sermon preparation and delivery. Second, Steven Paulson's *Lutheran Theology* is used as a secondary source for the impact of Forde's theology on preaching. Paulson is a student of Forde and extends many of his ideas throughout this volume. At the center of his argument is that the Lutheran Reformation is a preaching movement, rather than a branch of the church catholic. Third, the multi-author volume *Justification Is for Preaching* is used to further explore the practical ramifications of Forde's thought for preaching. This volume is a collection of several essays published in *Lutheran Quarterly* that touch upon the doctrine of justification and gospel proclamation from the pulpit. Though from a variety of writers, these various essays explain these issues in view of Forde's unique theological positions. These writers can all broadly be placed under the umbrella of "Radical Lutheranism."

Primary and Secondary Discourse

The central argument in Forde's work on preaching is that there is a vast difference between systematic theology and the act of proclamation. In his view, preaching has often neglected its proper role as proclamation as pastors have used the pulpit to give systematic theological lectures, ethical exhortation, or emotional appeals. To explain such a difference between these two acts, Forde distinguishes between primary and secondary discourse. Various elements of theologizing, such as the specific explication of doctrinal content or the discussion of ethical norms are categorized as secondary discourse. This type of discourse is language which speaks *about* God, grace, or various other theological topics. Primary discourse, in contrast to this, is not descriptive language, but speech which delivers what is says. This comes in the form of second-person address. Rather than speaking about God's love in the abstract, primary discourse gives that love with the declaration, "I love you." Forde purports that this type of language is not a sign which points elsewhere; it does not lead one to any ideas outside of itself. In this sense, Forde rejects the sign-signified language prevalent

Conclusion

in the Augustinian tradition.[1] While Forde does not reject the necessity of secondary discourse (to the contrary, he views it as a necessary corollary to proclamation), he argues that this is not the central element in preaching. The purpose of systematic theology is to enhance and encourage primary discourse.

The distinction between these two kinds of discourse is not one utilized in historic Lutheranism. This, in and of itself, does not negate the distinction, but such novelty must be recognized. In a sense, the distinction between the two types of discourse is a valid one. There is, of course, a linguistic differentiation between the declaration "I forgive you" and the statement "Jesus forgives the sins of the world." The first is a second-person declaration, whereas the latter is a third-person theological assertion. It also is certainly the case that there are specific instances in which the method of primary discourse is divinely commanded. The baptismal formula, the words of institution, and absolution include explicit "for you" language to the individual. This being said, there are two primary concerns with Forde's strong differentiation between these two modes of speech. First, Forde assumes that there is such a thing as language which does not point anywhere other than to itself. This simply is not the case. Any direct proclamation contains theological content. For the words "this is my body broken for you" to have any meaning to the individual who receives the Supper, some theological understanding of the nature of the sacrament is necessary. This is especially true from a Lutheran perspective, wherein the nature of Christ's presence in the Supper is a fundamental theological and practical concern. Similarly, the declaration "I forgive you" is full of theological content. Such an announcement assumes knowledge of what constitutes forgiveness, the nature of sin, the atonement, God's relationship

---

1. This distinction between Augustine's and Luther's theology of sign is not unique with Forde, but has been explored by a number of writers. Herman Sasse argues that Augustine set the groundwork for a Reformed approach to the sacraments, wherein the elements serve as mere signs that point elsewhere (Sasse, *We Confess*, 15–18). Though he acknowledges that Luther used language of signs, especially in his early writings, Sasse contends that eventually, Luther dropped such language, and he even summarizes Luther's reform as "the great overthrow of Augustinianism in the church" (ibid., 19). Chemnitz and the following Lutheran scholastics did consistently use the language of sign, however (Chemnitz, *Loci Theologici* 3:1361–62), while rejecting the Reformed divorce between the sign and thing signified. The problem identified by Forde and Sasse is not with the Augustinian distinction itself, but with the manner in which it has been interpreted by certain theological traditions. Perhaps most useful here would be Thomas's terminology of an "efficacious sign."

to sin, and several other ideas. One might respond that Forde does view secondary discourse as a necessary additional element to preaching. This much is true, as Forde consistently maintains the necessity of systematic theology. Even so, he consistently rejects the practice of systematic theology in any of its traditional forms, leaving one to wonder exactly what the content of genuine secondary-discourse theology is. Throughout *Theology Is for Proclamation*, he frames systematic theology as defined by the act of proclamation while rejecting traditional substance-ontology; again, act has precedence over being, and therefore, theological assertions must be grounded in the event of proclamation. This significantly alters the content of what is considered genuine systematic theology. Even if Forde were to accept that traditional systematic categories were correct, such a strong divide between these two modes of discourse is simply not possible. There must be systematic theological content within any second-person declaration if it is to have any coherency whatsoever.

The second problem with Forde's division between these two modes of discourse is that is does not accord with the biblical witness. For Lutheran orthodoxy, statements about both objective and subjective justification are identified as gospel. There are *historia salutis* and *ordo salutis* realities confined under the good news which one is called to preach. Kurt Marquart identifies the gospel stories themselves as sacraments, through which the historical reality of objective justification and the personal reception of subjective justification are united.[2] In his attempt to avoid the problems of historical criticism, Forde negates any extensive discussion about the historical reality of various elements of the biblical narrative and instead focuses on the eschatological event of redemption that occurs to the individual in the present. In both the preaching of Jesus and the sermons recorded in the book of Acts, statements about historical events and direct address to individuals are both identified as saving words. It is noteworthy that Forde rejects any strong connection between the Christ of history and the Christ of faith, and thus denies that Jesus attributed divine titles to himself prior to the resurrection. Thus, the preaching of Jesus as recorded in the Gospels may simply be a reflection of the developed theology of the church rather than the words of the historical person of Jesus himself. In this way, Forde adopts a type of form criticism as promoted by Bultmann. In perhaps the most famous text in the entire New Testament, Jesus points Nicodemus to the historical reality that God sent his Son into the world in order that all

---

2. Marquart, *Saving Truth*, 85.

Conclusion

who believe might be saved (John 3:16). The fact that Jesus did not declare this statement to Nicodemus in the mode of second-person address does not lessen the impact of Christ's words. If Forde is correct, then this is simply an instance of Jesus speaking "about the gospel" instead of doing actual proclamation. In the book of Acts, similarly, there are sermons, such as the one preached at the Areopagus (Acts 17:22–34), where no explicit "for you" proclamation is given, and yet some believe and are saved. Forde's strong preference of second-person discourse over third-person language arises not from an examination of the biblical text, but from his personalistic-eschatological theology.

Without exposure to Forde's central theological convictions as exposited throughout his writings, one might assume that the intent of this distinction between two types of discourse is simply to encourage the preacher not to speak in abstract categories, but in a manner accessible to the congregation. Forde's convictions here are driven by other ideological concerns, as addressed previously. The primary differentiating factor between Forde and the confessional Lutheran tradition, as has been explained, is the prioritization of act over being. His approach to preaching, like his view of the law, atonement, and other topics, is based upon this prioritization. Truths about God expressed through systematic theology are not the word of God, but simply words *about* God. The word of God only becomes such as it is directly addressed to the hearer. In this way, Forde is consistent with Barth's approach to the divine word not as a number of propositions on the pages of Scripture, but as an encounter between God and the sinner; Forde's uniqueness here is in his emphasis upon Scripture becoming the word of God through the proclamation of law and gospel, unlike Barth, who speaks of a single word of God that includes both promise and command. In this manner, Forde's theology of the word is a type of Lutheran Barthianism.

For Forde, Christian history has generally replaced primary discourse with secondary. This is not simply true prior to the Reformation, as Forde calls the sixteenth century a "temporary interruption" in the prioritization of secondary over primary discourse.[3] Steven Paulson affirms Forde's point and further contends that the history of Lutheran theology is "the story of attempts to being the law back into the Christian life."[4] Following the death of Martin Luther, theology gradually became associated with the academy rather than the pulpit, and this led to a neglect of proclamation. Instead of

---

3. Forde, *Theology Is for Proclamation*, 6.
4. Paulson, *Lutheran Theology*, 4.

preaching the gospel, Lutheran scholasticism only spoke *about* the gospel. In Forde's view, this neglect of proclamation remains in both the liberal and conservative branches of the church. Forde is highly critical of the doctrine of biblical inerrancy, as this causes the divine word to be "set in stone," to the neglect of the active and dynamic present power of God's word.[5] In this context, Forde acknowledges the validity of "Lessing's ditch," which separates the eternal truths of reason for the accidental truths of history. For Forde, such a dilemma is not solved through the proposition that Scripture is an infallible record of historical truths, but through the act of "for you" proclamation in the present, so that God's word does not remain a relic of past history. Forde views his perspective as an alternative approach to both conservative and liberal approaches to the relationship between Scripture and actual history. In reality, Forde simply adopts a liberal historical-critical methodology and uses his personalized-eschatology to simply avoid the consequences of such a conviction by divorcing theology from its historical content.

Forde's theology of preaching is highly dependent upon his dialectical methodology. Throughout his writings, Forde speaks in a dialectical mode and is generally skeptical of a theology which seeks some kind of logical or theological consistency. This is why he speaks of law and gospel in a polarizing manner and also continually relies on the hidden God–revealed God dichotomy. Historical Lutheranism is fond of utilizing various paradoxical themes, such as law and gospel, the two kingdoms, and the careful balance between *sola gratia* and *gratia universalis*. However, none of these ideas is explained as outright contradiction; the doctrine of divine simplicity assures that God is always consistent within himself. Forde, to the contrary, does not have any desire to reconcile these various theological ideas at all, instead simply allowing the tension to stand, not only as paradox, but seemingly as contradiction. This is consistent with the law-gospel polarity that Biermann contends is prevalent in contemporary Lutheranism.[6] In his theology of preaching, Forde proposes the utilization of another relatively unknown distinction in Luther's thought, that between God-preached and God-not-preached. His students further this distinction, and Paulson even calls it "the most important distinction Lutheran theology makes."[7] This idea is present in Luther's refutation of Erasmus in *The Bondage of the Will*.

---

5. Forde, *Theology Is for Proclamation*, 7.
6. Biermann, *Case for Character*, 116.
7. Paulson, *Lutheran Theology*, 23.

Conclusion

The question at issue is the interpretation of Ezekiel 18:23, in which God proclaims that he does not desire the death of the sinner. While Erasmus takes this as a general principle that God desires the salvation of all people in defense of his notion of free will, Luther notes that such a phrase is not an abstract universal truth, but speaks in Ezekiel's particular context to those the prophet was called to preach to. In other words, Luther viewed this statement as an instance of primary-discourse gospel proclamation, rather than secondary-discourse theologizing about the nature of God. Forde speaks of "God-not-preached" as any explanation of deity in the abstract. Any theological statements surrounding the attributes or essence of God does not foster proclamation and thus is not useful to the sinner. In contrast to this, one encounters salvation only through God-preached. Forde uses "God-preached" as a synonym for primary theological discourse. These are words which deliver forgiveness.

One problem that arises from Forde's approach is its disconnection from previous Christian history. In his view, this vital distinction between God-preached and God-not-preached has been discarded for the majority of the church's existence. Forde views such a loss as the result of Christian responses to early heretical gnostic views.[8] For the gnostic writers, the physical creation is identified with bondage, and salvation includes escape from the physical world. The church fathers attempted to reject this system by proposing a good creation from which the human race fell in Adam. To defend the goodness of man, even as fallen, they also argued that one's free will was left damaged, but not lost. Salvation therefore includes the cooperation of the human creature with divine grace. Lutheran orthodox writers would affirm part of Forde's argument here. Article II of the Formula of Concord defends the notion that the human creature's free will in regard to things "above us" is lost and is only recovered by divine grace. In other words, the Formula defends an Augustinian approach to the human will in opposition to the Pelagian and Semipelagian perspectives. In contrast to this, Forde does not simply defend an Augustinian position on the will. Rather, he rejects the entire scheme of original righteousness in the garden of Eden, the fall of a literal Adam and Eve, and God's consequent restoration of the human race to original innocence and blessedness. Such an obsession with God's historical acts denies the eschatological newness of the gospel as present in proclamation. Forde does not reject a historical fall *per se*, but he views such a question as ultimately unnecessary from the

---

8. Forde, *Theology Is for Proclamation*, 40.

perspective of proclamation.[9] The bondage of the will is not a reality which finds its place in either a redemptive historical or systematic theological system. Instead, it is an existential reality which comes about through encounter with God. The early Christian schema, whether taught by a Semipelagian or by Augustine, relegates salvation to doctrine and fails to uphold a proper understanding of the human condition and the act of salvation through proclamation.

Forde's view, then, according to his own reckoning, is a relative novelty within the church. This is clear in the manner in which Forde describes his approach to Christology. While he does not reject the Nicene or Chalcedonian definitions outright, Forde addresses several criticisms of the use of substance-ontology as definitional to Christology and Trinitarian theology. Rather than Christ as the combination of two substances, divine and human, he should be spoken of as God doing himself to us.[10] The category of substance may have been useful for a time, in order to defend against Arianism, but ultimately, such language must be put to an end just as the law is put to an end. Again, Forde's attempt to reconstruct Christology is based upon his rejection of categories of being for those of action. This fundamental redefinition of the entire theological task, and consequently preaching, has serious implications for the catholicity of the Lutheran faith from Forde's perspective. While he remains Trinitarian, and committed to the full divinity and humanity of Christ (though not necessarily in essentialist terms), Forde sets up his own theology as differentiated from the majority of the Christian world and the history of Christian theology. Since this all goes back to preaching, one wonders if the church has misunderstood the fundamental task of proclamation from its very beginning. The implication of Forde's argument is that a true and genuine proclamation of law and gospel has been absent throughout the history of the church, with relatively few exceptions—such as that of Luther and Forde himself.

The distinction made between primary and secondary discourse is not completely inconsistent with the orthodox Lutheran approach to law and gospel. As has been demonstrated through Pieper, Chemnitz, Gerhard, and the Formula of Concord, the distinction between law and gospel has never been a purely theoretical exercise, but is used to comfort contrite sinners and to terrify those who are secure in their sins. Preaching has always had an existential element, as God's word is not merely a composition of various

9. Ibid., 50–51.
10. Ibid., 100.

doctrines, but contains his commands and promises, through which the Holy Spirit convicts and sets free. In this sense, there is a genuinely beneficial way in which one can speak of the necessity of preaching the law and the gospel in a "for you" context, so that various doctrines do not remain abstract. This being said, however, Forde's use of this distinction within his personalistic-eschatological approach to theology is ultimately unhelpful. He divorces the importance of the preaching of specific theological content (which is often spoken of in terms of being rather than act) from the act of proclamation itself. Such a strong divorce has no scriptural warrant and may lead to a neglect of catechetical preaching. Ultimately, this approach separates Forde from the majority of Christian preachers and thinkers throughout history, and thus has profound implications for the catholicity of the Lutheran church. These problematic elements in Forde's approach are apparent in those writers who follow this tradition.

Radical Lutheran Preaching

The distinction made by Forde between primary and secondary discourse is explored in a number of ways through those writers and pastors who are part of the Radical Lutheran tradition. The identification of the preaching task with the primary-discourse reality of the second-person "for you" declaration that one is forgiven has several implications for the pastor in the Lutheran pulpit. These implications demonstrate some of the differences between Forde and the confessional Lutheran tradition, and consequently, the flaws in Forde's approach. While significantly more space could be devoted to the multitude of ways in which Forde's theology impacts preaching, four are addressed here. First, the Radical Lutheran approach to preaching distorts the biblical and confessional doctrine of election and places this act into the hands of the preacher himself rather than God in eternity past. Second, Forde's approach to preaching negates the necessity of the proclamation of God's law. In these writers, sin is spoken of almost exclusively as misunderstanding justification. Third, the Radical Lutheran and confessional Lutheran approaches to preaching differ in the manner in which the pastor speaks to those who are regenerated and converted. While the scholastic Lutherans affirm that the sinner's will is freed through grace, Forde fails to distinguish between the bondage of the will of the unregenerate and regenerate individuals. Finally, the Radical Lutheran approach neglects the importance of exegesis and catechesis in the preaching task.

The doctrine of predestination is likely not the first to come to mind when one considers the nature of the preaching task. For many in the Radical Lutheran tradition, however, preaching is the context in which election is to be placed. The doctrine of election is sometimes considered abstract or problematic even among the most eminent theologians. There has been extensive debate over the nature of election, especially within American Lutheranism; the Ohio and Iowa Synods separated from the Synodical Conference due to different approaches to the relationship of faith to eternal election.[11] However, despite the various differences among Lutheran theologians regarding the phrase "*intuitu fidei*" (the idea that one is elected *in view of* faith, rather than *unto* faith), there is a general consensus that election is an act of God in eternity past, wherein he decrees that specific individuals will be saved. Conrad Lindberg expresses the traditional Lutheran perspective through his contention that election is immutable, eternal, and irrevocable.[12] Though differentiated from the Calvinistic concept of an absolute predestination to both life and death, the scholastic Lutheran tradition places election within the context of eternity. This much might seem obvious in view of Paul's contention in Ephesians that such an act occurs "before the foundation of the world" (Eph 1:4), but this perspective is challenged by Forde, who instead places the act of election in the event of proclamation.

While it is Forde himself who proposes that there is a relationship between election and preaching, especially in his treatment of Luther's debate with Erasmus titled *The Captivation of the Will*, this idea has developed more thoroughly through his student Steven Paulson. In his book *Lutheran Theology*, Paulson presents a treatment of Lutheranism through the lens of preaching. For Paulson, Lutheranism itself is identified as primarily a preaching movement within the church, and Luther's revolution is principally related to the nature and function of Christian proclamation. Like Forde, Paulson consistently criticizes the Lutheran scholastic tradition, and most particularly, the idea of the law as God's eternal moral will. What is relevant to this discussion is Paulson's view of election. Throughout this volume, Paulson presents the pastor as the agent of election. Unlike the entire previous Lutheran tradition, he asserts that election is not an eternal act of God, whereby specific individuals are chosen unto salvation (whether in view of faith or not), but as the "for you" proclamation of the pastor in the

11. This debate is catalogued in Suelflow, *Servant of the Word*, 167–73.
12. Lindberg, *Christian Dogmatics*, 87.

Conclusion

present. Election, for Paulson, is essentially primary theological discourse and is identical with both the call and justification. He states, "Preachers do not come with information about an election done elsewhere, outside of time; preachers actually do the electing here and now, in the present."[13] This theological novelty has significant implications for the manner in which pastors view the preaching task.

Forde's metaphysical assumptions are at work in this divide between an eternal act of election and the present act of the preacher electing an individual. To speak about an eternal action on God's behalf is to move from the realm of act to that of being. Election is then a concept or series of ideas surrounding the nature of God's eternal decree, rather than a performative action in the present. It is thus consistent with Forde's system that a traditional perspective on predestination would be rejected, as it does not fit the criteria of proper systematic theological discourse, which is always a reflection on the proclamation itself. A traditional Lutheran sermon on predestination can be found in the Danish Lutheran Petrus Nakskow's *Articles of Faith of the Holy Evangelical Church*,[14] which is a compilation of sermons on numerous theological topics. Nakskow presents the topic first with a scriptural text, and then an exposition of that scriptural text. Following this, the Danish theologian discusses the various aspects of the doctrine of election, including its purpose, the content of such a teaching, the means of election, the ground of election, and so forth. Within this discussion, he includes several practical uses for the teaching and relates the Lutheran position to those held in the broader church. This type of preaching is standard in the age of Lutheran scholasticism. Such might seem like a basic approach to preaching on a doctrinal topic such as election. For Paulson, however, this misses the entire point of the doctrine of election. This teaching is not something to be spoken *about*, but something to actually be *accomplished* in the act of preaching. According to Paulson, a sermon like Nakskow's is inconsistent with Luther's own view, in which election is something actualized in proclamation.

If the fundamental task of the preacher is simply *doing* rather than *talking about* any particular theological topic, whether election or something else, the nature and content of proclamation drastically changes. Theologians like Nakskow are not faithful to the preaching task when preaching catechetical sermons that expound upon various systematic theological

13. Paulson, *Lutheran Theology*, 25.
14. Nakskow, *Articles of Faith*, 148–56.

topics. There are two fundamental issues with Paulson's contention here which must be addressed. First, Paulson conflates various events of the *ordo salutis* into one. Traditionally, predestination occurs in eternity past and is related to God's decree to save those who are to be his children. This predestination is enacted in time, but this event in time is not identified with election itself. One is predestined *unto* various elements of salvation, which are applied by the Holy Spirit in time. This includes the call, regeneration, justification, sanctification, and perseverance. What Paulson identifies with election, Lutheran scholastics label "the call," or *vocatio*. These are not mere semantic issues, but this is essential to a faithful exposition of the scriptural text. This leads to the second problem with Paulson's approach: it simply does not accord with Scripture. Paul exposits election as an event before the foundation of the world (Eph 1:4) and as identified with foreknowledge (Rom 8:29). There is no single instance in Scripture wherein election is identified as an act which occurs in time or which is the action of the preacher. It is apparent that such a teaching arises from underlying metaphysical convictions, and not from Scripture or the previous Lutheran (or catholic!) tradition.

Along with the problematic view of election in Radical Lutheran preaching, Forde's theology also fails to give a necessary place to the law in the pulpit. As was demonstrated, Forde speaks about the necessity of law, but at the same time, he redefines law so that it has no specific reference to the divine commands. Consequently, there is no necessary import of the law in its historic sense in preaching at all. Again, this is not to say that Forde promotes licentiousness, or that he views ethics as completely fruitless. However, one might get this impression when listening to the preaching of someone who comes from Forde's perspective. This is demonstrated by a read of Forde's own sermons, which hardly mention specific commandments at all. A practical example of this is found in Virgil Thompson's article "Preaching the Justification of Zacchaeus," first published in *Lutheran Quarterly*, and included in the volume *Justification Is for Preaching*. This article serves as an example of how Forde's theology applies to preaching a specific text and explains how this methodology is to be used in formulating the content of one's sermon. The article is not all worthy of critique, as several elements of Thompson's argument accord with Lutheran orthodoxy, such as his rejection of various moralistic interpretations of the story of Zacchaeus. However, alongside a helpful exposition of the tax collector's

Conclusion

free salvation given by Christ, Thompson demonstrates several shortcomings of the Radical Lutheran approach to Christian preaching.

The first thing to note is that Thompson characterizes the entire task of the minister as the proclamation of justification. Now, certainly, in Lutheran orthodoxy the doctrine of justification holds a central position in a manner that it does not in other theological traditions, such as the Reformed or Roman Catholic. This is why A. G. Voigt, in his *Biblical Dogmatics*, discusses justification prior to the *ordo salutis* in order to emphasize its theological priority.[15] However, for these writers, justification is not the *only* content of theology. There are certain genuine theological questions which the doctrine of justification is not meant to answer. A good example of this reductionism is in Thompson's characterization of the Christian preacher as one who is a "flesh-and-blood sinner," who is justified solely by grace.[16] Now, certainly, there is truth to this characterization, as all Christians remain both sinners and saints prior to death. However, in Radical Lutheran writings, this reality is basically the *only* thing said about the nature of the Christian preacher. This approach is reductionistic, as it fails to faithfully exposit the various scriptural texts which list moral qualifications for the Christian minister. A read of Thompson, Bayer (whom Thompson frequently cites in this essay), and others gives the impression that the *only* qualification for pastoral ministry is a recognition that one is a sinner. In their respective treatments of the doctrine of the ministry, Chemnitz and Gerhard both speak about the necessity of the moral life for the one who is placed into the pastoral office. Two significant nineteenth-century Lutheran theologians, C. F. W. Walther and George Henry Gerberding, spend an extensive amount of space in their pastoral theology textbooks on such issues. Again, Forde and other writers in this tradition would not likely deny the benefit of a virtuous minister, but any discussion of this is absent in their writings.

The solution to this problem is to utilize Biermann's distinction between the two kinds of righteousness as a faithful exposition of Luther's thought. By distinguishing between the *coram Deo* and *coram mundo* spheres, one has the proper theological categories in which to place the two realities of the Christian minister. *Coram Deo*, Thompson is correct that like all other human creatures prior to the eschaton, even the greatest pastor remains a sinner, and his justification is established solely by faith.

---

15. Voigt, *Biblical Dogmatics*, 165.
16. Thompson, *Justification Is for Preaching*, 250.

However, *coram mundo*, there is a necessity for virtuous living in order for one to be prepared for the pastoral office. Thus, one need not ignore Paul's requirement of blamelessness (1 Tim 3:2) because of some encroachment upon justification *coram Deo*. Blamelessness before God is an impossibility on the basis of one's moral life. However, *coram mundo*, one can indeed be blameless, and this is what is expected of one in the pastoral office.

The second flaw in Thompson's treatment of preaching is his contention that its sole purpose is the existential impact of the gospel on the hearer as an instrument of death and life. He explicitly states that justification is not "just one theme among others," but is the only content of Christian sermons.[17] He is reliant on Forde's distinction between primary and secondary discourse, as Thompson contends that justification is not merely to be talked about, but to be accomplished in proclamation. Again, he is not completely inconsistent with confessional Lutheranism on this point. Certainly, Lutheran theologians have emphasized the centrality of the gospel, and of justification in particular, in preaching. However, they never limit the impact of preaching to the doing of justification, as they also emphasize the importance of ethical exhortation, catechesis, and other elements of the sermon. Pieper notes that a proper understanding of justification leads ministers to proclaim the necessity of good deeds.[18] It is also the case that law and gospel both serve as instruments of death and life, and the law continues its second function upon the believer through preaching. What Thompson argues here, however, is not that the law brings death and the gospel brings life; it is the act of *justification* which is identified with death and life. This arises from Forde's treatment of the doctrine of justification in *Justification: A Matter of Life and Death*, wherein he argues that justification is not a forensic declaration, but the death and resurrection of the sinner. If it is not the law, but justification itself, which has a killing function upon the sinner, then the law essentially has no purpose at all. This is consistent with Forde's contention that sin is recognized by the unconditional nature of gospel proclamation, rather than an explicit exposition of God's commandments.

The third problem in Thompson's essay is in his actual exposition of the story of Zacchaeus. He does, rightfully, respond to some common interpretations of this text which base Jesus' interest in Zacchaeus upon some action or worthiness on Zacchaeus' part. Such expositors neglect to

---

17. Ibid.
18. Pieper, *Christian Dogmatics* 3:49.

Conclusion

understand the unconditional nature of Jesus' relationship to the tax collector.[19] Zacchaeus is not seeking Jesus, but Jesus instead seeks Zacchaeus. The problem in Thompson's treatment of this story is in his approach to the law in this text. He does not speak about the sins which characterized Zacchaeus' life prior to his conversion, such as cheating and greed. Instead, the problem Jesus solves is Zacchaeus' desire for self-justification as taught by "conditional theologians."[20] Thompson acknowledges that the text itself gives no indication that Zacchaeus was a self-righteous man seeking his own justification, but then he dismisses the lack of exegetical grounding for his argument by saying, "it takes one to know one."[21] In other words, we all seek self-justification, and therefore, Zacchaeus did too. This is the most glaring issue with Thompson's essay, but also with Radical Lutheran preaching in general. The figure in this text is guilty of explicit sins as related to his role as a tax collector. However, rather than giving an exposition of how these sins are a violation of God's specific commandments, Thompson imports into the story the sin of "self-justification," which is nowhere in the text itself. In reality, according to this reading, the gospel does not set one free from the law at all—at least in any traditional sense—but from one's desire for self-justification. This is commensurate with Forde's perspective on sanctification as "getting used to justification." If self-justification is *the* human problem, then both justification and renewal are intimately connected with solving this particular problem. Although Radical Lutheran theologians speak about law and gospel, the preaching of many of these writers does not really include the law at all.

It is important to note that not all writers who might be described as part of the Radical Lutheran tradition neglect the proclamation of specific divine commandments. The movement itself is far from monolithic, as these writers are unified primarily in their adherence to certain theological convictions that arise from Forde's writings. James Nestingen, for example, is a frequent contributor to *Lutheran Quarterly*, but he explicitly makes the distinction between the law's essence and office.[22] In this way, Nestingen rejects the fundamental theological tenet of Forde's work. It would be unfair to accuse him of failing to exposit specific commandments in preaching, as such is demonstrably not the case. Similarly, Mark Mattes is more careful

---

19. Thompson, *Justification Is for Preaching*, 254.
20. Ibid., 257.
21. Ibid.
22. Ibid., 233.

about his explanation of the law than Forde, Paulson, or Thompson. These writers are closer to the confessional Lutheran tradition than some others in the movement. It is also worth noting that there are some Missouri Synod theologians who are highly influenced by Forde's unique theological convictions. The two most prominent writers in this vein are Robert Kolb and John T. Pless. Again, while someone might label them "Radical Lutherans," they exposit the law in a clear manner and are not guilty of the kinds of reductionism found in some authors. Such a treatment as this—which focuses more particularly on Forde himself—is not capable of the nuance necessary to exposit the various perspectives of each writer.

The third major problem in the preaching methodology promoted by Gerhard Forde is that there is no explicit distinction between the human person prior to conversion and after conversion. Forde and the scholastic Lutheran tradition both emphasize the bondage of the will, as taught in Luther's famous treatise. Insofar as both traditions address the unregenerate individual, there is agreement surrounding the inability of free will to choose that which is spiritually good. The unbeliever is, instead, in bondage to sin. For the Radical Lutheran, however, when one preaches the gospel, one is *always* preaching to a bound will. In his essay "Categorical Preaching," Paulson argues that there is no neutrality of the will whatsoever. This is not a statement about the nature of the human being as a sinner prior to conversion, but as a general truth. Furthermore, Paulson then notes that proclamation is always "*preaching to the dead.*"[23] The uniqueness of Christian preaching lies specifically in the reality that its purpose is to continue to raise the dead. In contrast to this, the Formula of Concord (Article II) distinguishes between the nature of the will before and after conversion. The bondage of the will is a reference to the fact that, through the sin of Adam, the human race is enslaved to sinful desire. Apart from God's gracious intervention, such enslavement would continue for the entirety of a person's life. However, God has given the means of grace (here, baptism and the word) in order to convert the person and grant liberty to the human will. Through regeneration, the Christian's will is freed so that he *can* now choose the good. In this way, there is a kind of synergism in Christian sanctification. This is not to say that the Christian's will has been *perfectly* freed, as the struggle with sin continues until death, but there is a measure of genuine freedom given to the human person. This difference constitutes

---

23. Ibid., 142.

Conclusion

an important divergence between Gerhard Forde and the confessional Lutheran tradition.

There are a number of problems with the contention that preaching is always a proclamation to the dead. First, and most importantly, this simply is not in accord with the biblical witness. It is in Paul's theology that the concept of deadness in sin is exposited as a major theme. He treats this in the second chapter of Ephesians, wherein it is said that Christians were dead in sins, but are no longer are (Eph 2:1). This deadness in sins corresponds to walking according to the sinful flesh rather than the Spirit. He continues to explain that the Ephesians have *already* been made alive in Christ, have become partakers of his resurrection, and have been seated in the heavenly realms with Christ (Eph 2:4–5).[24] There simply are no exegetical grounds for the contention that preaching is always directed toward those who are spiritually dead. Paul's own writing indicates that the proclamation of Christian truth to those who are converted and to those who are not differs.

This demonstrates, again, that the traditional dogmatic category of the bondage of the will has been replaced by an existential theme. The Lutheran orthodox describe the nature of the human will in a variety of ways.[25] In the state of integrity, prior to the fall, Adam and Eve had the freedom to either sin or not sin. This state no longer exists due to the consequences of original sin. Through the loss of original righteousness, human beings are then placed into a state of bondage. Humans have freedom in civil matters, but spiritually, they are enslaved to sin. Through regeneration, the will is freed to choose the good, though not entirely without sin. This is called the "state of reparation,"[26] wherein eschatological freedom from sin is anticipated.

---

24. In his book *Resurrection and Redemption*, Richard Gaffin explores the theme of the individual's resurrection in connection with Christ's own resurrection throughout Paul's theology. He demonstrates that there is an intimate connection between Christ's death and resurrection as redemptive historical events and the individual's experience of death and resurrection in the *ordo salutis*. The believer experiences a "co-crucifixion" with Christ, and consequently receives the vindication Christ obtained through his resurrection. Gaffin argues that the "deadness in sin" in Eph 2 is a reference to moral depravity apart from regeneration. Resurrection is then presented as the solution to this dilemma, wherein one is transformed—in dogmatic language, this is a reference to regeneration. This co-resurrection occurs in the individual believer's life as a past experience, wherein one participates in Christ's own resurrection. The believer then lives life as one who *has already* been raised, in anticipation of the eschatological resurrection from death (Gaffin, *Resurrection and Redemption*, 41–43). For Paulson to prove his case, it would have to be demonstrated that such a reading is mistaken. Thus far, this has not been done.

25. Schmid, *Doctrinal Theology*, 257–62.

26. Ibid., 268.

This state is that of all believing, baptized Christians, and thus constitutes the majority of those people who hear the proclamation of the word in an average worship service. The idea that preaching is always directed toward those who are spiritually dead is completely inconsistent with the traditional Lutheran view. This is not a development in the later Protestant scholastic era, but these distinctions are spoken of in the Formula of Concord (FC SD II.67). Radical Lutherans reject this entire scheme because in Forde's view, the bondage of the will is an existential reality of what happens when one is confronted by the unconditional gospel promise. It is not a redemptive-historical or dogmatic category. Though the language of the two interpretations of the Lutheran tradition appears similar, the underlying concepts in each differ, resulting in two different approaches to preaching.

The final aspect of Forde's approach to Lutheran preaching which is detrimental to the pastoral task is the lack of exegetical and catechetical teaching from the pulpit. Since older Lutheran theologians did not distinguish between primary and secondary discourse, there was no intentional move to prioritize a "for you" gospel proclamation to the neglect of catechetical elements in preaching. Preaching like that of Petrus Nakskow, who has an entire dogmatic theology comprised of sermons, simply does not fit into the framework for preaching that Forde formulates. For Forde, a sermon which expounds upon a specific doctrinal point is misguided, as it is language "about the gospel" rather than the gospel itself. One would not, then, preach a sermon on the topic of vicarious atonement that explains the biblical, theological, and practical implications of such a teaching. Instead, the cross must be proclaimed as an existential reality that does something to the hearer. In essence, the sermon—for the Radical Lutheran—is nothing more than an extended absolution, as it is foundationally (and some say *solely*!) a proclamation of justification that kills and raises to life. If this is the case, one might wonder if there is any purpose in the preaching task at all, when the absolution itself performs the same task in a more succinct and direct manner.

A good example of the practical implications of this approach to preaching is the book *A Lutheran Primer for Preaching*, by Edward O. Grimenstein. This short volume is a guide to Lutheran preaching by a pastor in the Lutheran Church—Missouri Synod and adjunct professor of homiletics at Concordia Seminary. Because he is a member of the LCMS, one might not expect to discover Forde's influence within his writing, due to his church's adherence to the Formula of Concord. As a confessional Lutheran,

Conclusion

Grimenstein does believe in the third use of the law and other doctrinal convictions which differentiate him from Forde. However, despite these disagreements, Grimenstein adopts Forde's fundamental convictions regarding the distinction between teaching and proclamation, and thus writes a textbook which guides preachers in sermon preparation from that particular perspective.

This volume begins with an extended discussion about the nature of speech, as Grimenstein criticizes the Western tradition of language as a symbol which points elsewhere. Instead, he argues that God's word is performative as law and gospel, and the performative nature of the word defines the preaching task. He summarizes the purpose of his book as an attempt to define preaching as active rather than representational speech. This is similar to Forde's distinction between the two modes of discourse. Throughout this work, he distinguishes between the task of preaching and that of Bible study. In a study, one might discuss specific theological content, grammatical issues in the text, and other matters pertaining to the nature of a biblical text. In his view, a sermon should consist in God's doing of his words to the hearers, rather than the preacher's own theological or textual exposition of a passage. This is simply a false dichotomy; God acts in and through theological and exegetical explanation, as these *are* means to proclaim law and gospel. It is certainly true that there is a difference between a Bible study and Christian preaching. In a Bible study, one has the ability to answer questions and give more historical and exegetical background to any given passage or topic of discussion. However, this distinction has been overemphasized to the point that any exegetical discussion or theological explication is dismissed from preaching as a distraction from the divine speech-act. A quick read through any older compendium of Lutheran sermons, such as those of C. F. W. Walther, demonstrates that such a divide is not taught by earlier theologians. John Fritz, in his classic work *Pastoral Theology*, argues that the exposition of correct Christian doctrine is in fact the most important aspect of preaching.[27] All other aspects of the sermon, including rebuke and comfort, arise from this function. Fritz cites Walther as stating that a sermon that exhorts and comforts without doctrinal instruction has failed in its purpose. This idea is founded, according to Fritz, upon the book of Romans, which includes eleven chapters of doctrinal exposition, only then followed by practical application. Lutheran theologian J. Michael Reu even argues that some sermons should consist

---

27. Fritz, *Pastoral Theology*, 71.

purely of doctrinal instruction.[28] In contrast to this, for Grimenstein, it is not doctrine but the act of absolution that serves as a model for how the preaching task is to be exercised. This is explained through a sermon worksheet that Grimenstein prepares to guide pastors in crafting messages.

Grimenstein presents this "sermon preparation worksheet" as a guide for one writing a sermon to be preached at a Lutheran worship service. The worksheet is divided into three sections, modeling a Trinitarian structure. The first statement relates to God the Father, and it simply states, "God is the Actor." The opening assumption is that the sermon itself is a divine speech-act through which God the Father does the gospel to those listening. Act is privileged over being and objective theological content. Grimenstein argues that every sermon should have a theme sentence, and this theme sentence must always be a declarative one.[29] The focus of the sermon is always on what God does through the act of proclamation, and never what the listener is called to do. Such a contention is hard to substantiate either scripturally or historically. The contention that for God's word to be efficacious it must be spoken in a declarative manner is an absolute novelty within Christian history. As cited above, there are numerous examples of biblical speech and preaching which communicate the gospel without being directly "declarative" in nature.

Also, an examination of the theological forefathers of Grimenstein's own Lutheran Church—Missouri Synod demonstrate that they themselves do not properly (according to his perspective) utilize the "for you" nature of gospel proclamation. Walther, throughout his sermons, is fond of utilizing a particular thematic structure. He introduces the theme by way of a particular question (sometimes a statement), and then presents two answers to that question which are expanded throughout the message. For example, on one Reformation Sunday, Walther asks the question, "Why Should We Not Be Ashamed of Luther's Name Which We Bear?," to which he gives the following response: "To answer this question I will show you: 1. why this is our duty, and 2. in what manner we must carry out this duty of ours."[30] This sermon does not accord with Grimenstein's model of preaching in two ways. First, the theme is not declarative at all, but is given in the form of question and answer. Grimenstein argues that using a question as a thematic

---

28. Ibid., 72.
29. Ibid., 82.
30. Walther, *Our Master's Table*, 120.

Conclusion

element leads to moralism.[31] Second, God's action is not mentioned at all in the question or its two answers. This is not only true of the introduction, however, but Walther does not make one declarative gospel statement in the entire sermon, which instead emphasizes one's duty to remain faithful to the gospel. This is not a rarity in his sermons, but messages like this extend throughout Walther's career. Walther himself is not unique here, either, but this same approach to preaching was the norm in nineteenth-century Lutheranism. If Grimenstein is correct, a more thorough argument and explanation of both Scripture and Lutheran history is merited in order that a speech-act–driven approach to proclamation be demonstrated historically, and most importantly, biblically.

What is perhaps most significant in Grimenstein's treatment is the nature of the questions that he proposes must be asked by a minister when preparing a sermon on any given text. Throughout, there is no attention given to the historical, theological, or thematic content of a scriptural passage, as he limits his exposition to the nature of the proclamation of law and gospel as instruments of death and life. The threefold outline he gives contains these three sections: God is the actor, Jesus is our redeemer, and the Holy Spirit works faith. The first section includes the declarative "theme sentence" addressed previously. The second section encourages ministers to determine how Jesus' work of salvation is described in this text, and particularly how the gospel is presented "for you." The third element, about the Holy Spirit, is limited to the Spirit's role of giving and strengthening faith. The minister is asked to discover how the people are "encouraged to believe in the works of God" in the text.[32] The problem here is not so much in terms of what is included in this outline, but what it *excluded*. In historic Lutheran preaching, the most important concern when expositing a given text is the nature of the text itself. Questions which might be asked here are, What is the context of the passage? What is the historical and theological background that the author uses when writing this text? What genre is the text in question? Are there grammatical issues which might affect one's interpretation of this text? What are the primary theological and practical concerns of this passage? Without these basic questions being answered, the practical applications of law and gospel in any given text are impossible to present. Grimenstein's methodology excludes the actual content of the text itself, so that one is in a position to import the law-gospel

---

31. Grimenstein, *Primer for Preaching*, 83.
32. Ibid., 110.

schema into every biblical passage, rather than allowing the text itself to drive preaching. Furthermore, in his approach to the application of a biblical text, Grimenstein leaves no room whatsoever for ethical exhortation. In the five-page sermon outline he presents, Grimenstein only speaks about the law as an introductory aspect of the sermon presented prior to the declarative proclamation of the gospel.[33] In this approach, law and gospel is not simply a structure used to distinguish between God's commands and promises. Instead, it serves as a sermon outline. The structure of preaching as presenting law followed by gospel guides the sermon, rather than the content and context of the text itself. It also leaves no place for exhortation unto good works in view of the gospel, as the work of the Holy Spirit is limited to the strengthening of faith. Ultimately, this approach to preaching limits the preacher's role to the declaration of law and gospel and neglects the essential role of exegesis and catechesis in the preaching task.

Theologians following Forde and the confessional Lutheran tradition present alternative approaches to the preaching task which have profound implications on the life of the church. For Forde and Paulson, the sermon is an act of election, whereby God works his choice for the salvation of individuals in time. This is an element of the sermon as a declaratory act through which God is the actor. In the confessional approach, election refers to an action of God in eternity past, wherein individuals are predestined unto salvation. Through preaching, God calls sinners to faith and repentance, but this is not identical to the act of election, but instead is a *result* of election. Forde emphasizes the condemnatory nature of God's law, but he does not give a proper place to a clear exposition of the divine commandments in preaching. Often, writers in this tradition speak of sin solely in terms of a desire for self-justification. Confessional Lutheranism emphasizes the law as a reflection of God's own eternal will, and preaching then includes the exposition of specific commandments as guided by the text. Forde and Paulson's view of the bondage of the will also differentiates itself from the Lutheran scholastics. For Radical Lutherans, all people are in bondage, including those who are regenerate. Preaching is an act of God's raising the dead. For the Lutheran scholastics, the redeemed individual is not in bondage to sin, and though sin continues throughout life, one's will is freed to choose the good. The dead are raised through regeneration, which is a past reality in the life of a believer. Finally, these two traditions diverge in the nature of catechesis and the structure of sermons. Due to

33. Ibid., 87.

Conclusion

their emphasis on the declarative speech-act, Radical Lutherans argue that the doing of justification is at the center of the task of preaching, and they neglect emphasis on exegesis and catechesis. In confessional Lutheran treatments on preaching, exegesis, catechesis, and practical application of law and gospel are all emphasized as necessary to sermon preparation and delivery. These differences are further explored below through the divergent approaches to ethics and Christian obedience as promoted by these two traditions.

Ethics and Spiritual Formation

Along with the practical variances in preaching, Forde and the confessional Lutheran tradition differentiate themselves in their approach to the ethical life. It is not the case that Forde views ethics as irrelevant or unimportant, but his theological convictions consistently lead to a rejection of ethical discussion and discourse from the pulpit, catechesis, and the theological task. Confessional Lutheranism has a rich ethical tradition, as numerous volumes on the subject have been published by Lutheran writers in various centuries. This discussion is largely dependent on the conviction that the law functions not only to condemn, but as a guide for ethical decision-making. These divergent approaches to the third use of the law, as well as the nature of preaching, lead to some important practical differences between these traditions.

There are a number of important issues raised by Forde's theology that relate to the nature of ethics in the Christian life, and not all of them can be adequately addressed here. Therefore, three specific areas will be discussed in relation to the ethical life. First, drawing on the previous section, the place of the inculcation of moral living in preaching will be addressed. Further implications are drawn out that have been developed in relation to Forde's perspective on the third use of the law as well as the sermon structure presented by Grimenstein. These ideas are not only relevant to the pulpit, but also to the pastor's daily catechetical work. Second, the idea of virtue will be addressed in Forde's theology as well as in contemporary developments within the confessional Lutheran tradition. While Forde rejects language about virtue as a significant theological concept, other Lutherans argue that this is an essential category to be discussed in view of one's various *coram mundo* relationships. Finally, the nature of the two kinds of righteousness as a framework for ethical formation will be explored in light of the differences between Forde and the confessional Lutheran tradition.

Forde himself did not write a preaching manual, and thus it is impossible to find a particular place in Forde's own writings wherein he exposits one particular sermon structure to be used to the exclusion of all others. However, several ideas inherent within his own thought and an examination of his own sermons lead to a general structure of sermon preparation and delivery which are consistent with Radical Lutheran theology. The Grimenstein text, examined above, though from a more confessional perspective than that of Forde, demonstrates some of the consistent applications of Forde's thought in relation to the structure of a sermon, which relates to the proper place of ethical formation in preaching. For Forde, the sermon in essence is an extended absolution, as direct primary discourse statements dominate in the pulpit. Again, the purpose is not simply to speak "about" the law and the gospel, but to deliver them concretely to the hearer. This being the case, there is simply no significant place for ethical discourse from the pulpit. Perhaps this would be an element of secondary discourse which may have a subservient role in proclamation, but an examination of Forde's own sermons demonstrates that such topics are rarely discussed. When issues of sin and obedience *are* addressed, they tend to be related to the nature of one's belief in justification rather than specific ethical commands. This is clear in Thompson's treatment of the Zacchaeus story exposited previously. Grimenstein's proposed sermon structure leaves no place whatsoever for ethical formation in Christian proclamation, as the law is only proclaimed as a precursor to the gospel, and the role of the Holy Spirit is limited to the strengthening of faith. The issues of ethical discourse and Christian proclamation have not gone unnoticed by contemporary Lutheran theologians, who have offered various proposals to ensure that exhortations unto obedience are to be included in sermons.

Biermann recognizes this problem in the beginning of his book *A Case for Character*. As a pastor himself, Biermann has struggled with the ramifications of a law-gospel–reductionist schema in his own preaching and demonstrates the shortcomings of this approach. In the introduction to his study of virtue ethics and the two kinds of righteousness, Biermann explains the practical problem he has diagnosed in certain strands of contemporary Lutheranism. He gives a theoretical scenario in which a pastor preaches a series of sermons through the book of Colossians, and in the third chapter he approaches a passage that includes various ethical

Conclusion

exhortations in relation to one's earthly relationships. In this scenario, the pastor is intent on preaching a strict law-gospel sermon, and in doing this, he is bound to speak of these exhortations only in the sense that the listeners are not able to obey them, which is then resolved in the proclamation of the gospel which finishes the sermon. According to Biermann, this is done in contradiction to the actual tone and meaning of the text itself. This illustration serves as an example of the type of preaching which is necessitated by law-gospel reductionism.[34] Kilcrease criticizes Biermann on this point for merely giving a theoretical circumstance about Lutheran preaching, which in his view, does not accord with reality.[35] This criticism is mistaken. The preaching outline explained by Grimenstein is an example of a model of preaching which could, in fact, only utilize this text from Colossians in the manner Biermann explains. He leaves absolutely no room for a thorough exposition of one's duties in this world without immediately following such admonition with the reality that everyone falls short in this area, and then offering a consequent exposition of the gospel. This is simply the logical conclusion of Forde's personalistic-eschatological perspective.

Biermann is not alone in his criticism of a strict law-gospel model of preaching. In his essay "Revisiting the Law-Gospel Paradigm in Light of the Old Testament," Scott Ashmon argues that the scriptural patterns of preaching are multifaceted. He criticizes interpretations of Luther which contend that the law-gospel distinction constitutes a strict sermon structure in which the message should be divided into first, law, and then second, gospel. In contrast to this, Ashmon argues that—in accord with Walther's approach—the sermon should include the "frequent interplay between law and gospel" which takes a number of different forms.[36] This is not to say that the sermon should never follow a law-then-gospel pattern, but this is not a sort of unchangeable standard in sermon writing. Ashmon demonstrates that, in the Old Testament, a variety of patterns are set forth relating to the precise order of law and gospel. He notes that it is a frequent occurrence in Scripture for grace to be the first word to an individual, which is then followed by exhortation. This pattern is developed in Genesis, wherein Adam is created by grace, and is then given the command to be fruitful and multiply. This is not merely a prelapsarian pattern, but it is echoed in the story of Abraham as well as the giving of the Ten Commandments.

---

34. Biermann, *Case for Character*, 1.
35. Kilcrease, "*Case for Character*," 85.
36. Ashmon, "Law-Gospel Paradigm," 3.

Ashmon further points out that there are also examples in Scripture of a law-gospel-law structure, as well as grace-law-grace. The point is that one must let the actual content and structure of the text itself determine how it is preached, rather than enforcing a particular preaching pattern onto each text. In his words, this "lets Scripture direct the form and function of the sermon," rather than placing every text into a preconceived structure.[37] This type of approach diverges from Grimenstein's strict law-gospel pattern and is more faithful to the text itself.

David Scaer, similarly, has contended for the necessity of ethical proclamation from the pulpit in contrast to some law-gospel–reductionist approaches. In his essay "Finding a Place for the Third Use of the Law in Our Preaching," Scaer proposes that the third use of the law is an essential theological category, and that it should inform Christian proclamation from a confessional perspective. He outlines the effects of Elert's rejection of the third use of the law in the contemporary church and notes that this move has shaped the past half century of Lutheran preaching, including some within the LCMS and other confessional church bodies. Some have concluded that the third use is only the second function of the law as applied to Christians. On this point, Scaer affirms Gerhard's position as he defines the third use of the law solely as a *positive* function. Scaer then provides some important theological observations to guide pastors in the proclamation of ethical norms in accord with the law's third use. He argues that there is both Christological and eschatological import to the law's third function. The ethical norms expressed in the divine law do not stand as some kind of independent created thing apart from God, but are a reflection of his own essence, and consequently, of Christ. In looking at the law, one sees the nature of Christ, and his own life. Thus, ethics must always be preached Christologically. This differentiates Christian ethical proclamation from that of pagan philosophers. The third function is also eschatological, as the positive use of the law works in anticipation of its final use in eternity. When the sin nature is stripped away, one will only see the law in a positive manner as it no longer accuses. This also corresponds to the function of God's commandments in the prelapsarian state. These theological observations demonstrate the flaws in Grimenstein's approach—as taken from Forde—wherein the law is proclaimed in a solely negative context.

Forde's approach to ethics and preaching stands in stark contrast to the confessional theology of proclamation. While some confessional

37. Ibid., 4.

Conclusion

writers, such as Grimenstein, have adopted a similar approach to Forde, many others have noted the inherent weaknesses in the Radical Lutheran perspective. While the gospel is certainly central to the preaching task, this does not negate the clear exposition of ethical norms as guided by the divine law. Law and gospel should not be approached as a strict sermon structure, but instead should be distinguished in a sermon in accord with the actual structure and content of any given text. This allows the minister, as in Biermann's illustration, to expound upon one's duty in human relationships when the text calls for it. It also leaves room for the various sermon structures inherent in both Testaments, as Ashmon argues. Finally, it allows for one to speak about the law in its third function in a proper, and positive, theological context which mirrors the life of Christ and the eschatological state, as Scaer demonstrates.

The second point to be examined in Forde's thought is his view of virtue in relation to other Lutheran approaches to the subject. His writing on virtue and ethics, along with those of Steven Paulson, demonstrate that there is no extensive space in this theological system for an emphasis or in-depth analysis of the moral life. The task of theology is divorced from that of ethics, as Forde is particularly skeptical of the Aristotelian virtue model; this is in opposition to the eschatological nature of God's justifying word. In contrast to this, the confessional Lutheran tradition has consistently utilized language of virtue. This is true of the confessional documents themselves, older Lutheran writers, and contemporary theologians. Here, these ideas are explored and contrasted. Ultimately, it is the confessional approach which allows one to speak in a biblical manner about virtue and ethical norms.

Forde's aversion to ethical discussion is apparent in his treatment of the Christian life in the second volume of Braaten and Jenson's *Christian Dogmatics*. In this text, Forde writes the entire locus on the Christian life, which includes the following four topics: Justification, Justification and Sanctification, Justification and This World, and Justification Today.[38] The titles of these sections themselves demonstrate a divergence from previous Lutheran tradition. For the scholastics, a treatment of the Christian life covers the entirety of the *ordo salutis* rather than a myopic emphasis on justification alone. This includes sanctification and good works—which Forde generally neglects in this text. He presents the Christian life as the unilateral action of God upon the believer, and specifically through the act

---

38. Braaten, *Christian Dogmatics* 2:393–469.

of death and life which Forde identifies as justification. He does, certainly, note that the moral life is important, but he states that the Christian life "is not immediately concerned with ethics as such, with specific counsel about actions to be taken in concrete situations."[39] The theologian is not concerned with particular moral questions, but instead with the granting of new life through the justifying word. It is only when the sinful creature is made new that he can then be open to the moral life in the world for the good of others. What Forde promotes is a view of pure spontaneity with regard to good works. The preacher is not to emphasize specific moral commands, nor does catechetical teaching have such a role. The good works of a believer are purely spontaneous, rather than coerced, and thus there is no focus on effort within the moral life. Biermann labels this the "Law and Gospel" framework for expounding upon Christian ethics, wherein the death-life impact of law and gospel overshadows explicit moral instruction. He rightly describes such a framework as inadequate for the moral life.[40]

It must be noted, in opposition to Forde, that Scripture itself gives explicit moral commandments in a variety of instances. Language about the cultivation of virtue is similarly used (2 Pet 1:5), which does not accord with Forde and Paulson's rejection of virtue ethics. The divide Forde proposes between the task of the theologian as that of proclamation and the questions of ethics is simply not supported by the scriptural text itself. Discussions of redemption and of the moral life are intimately connected in both Testaments. Forde simply does not adequately address the textual evidence that demonstrates his perspective to be mistaken. Were the New Testament authors content to simply proclaim the gospel with no ethical instruction following the word of forgiveness, they would have done so. Such is simply not the case. Furthermore, Forde's divide here neglects the moral and ethical dialogue which has been part of the theological and catechetical task of the church from its beginnings. What Forde offers here is a complete revision of Christian theology and practice which is inconsistent with the catholicity of the church.

Forde's approach to the ethical life is further exposited through his treatment of Luther's *simul iustus et peccator* principle. While Forde usually speaks of this idea in a *totus-totus* manner, at one point he acknowledges that Luther occasionally speaks of the Christian as *part* saint and *part* sinner. Such a truth might seem to contradict Forde's claims that there is no

---

39. Ibid., 397.
40. Biermann, *Case for Character*, 115.

Conclusion

progressive sanctification in the traditional sense. However, he posits a solution to this dilemma which is consistent with his theological program. For Forde, there is a kind of progress in the Christian life. However, such progress is different from how it is often understood. Forde is particularly critical of Aristotle's approach to virtue ethics, wherein through habituation, one can become gradually more virtuous through human effort. In Forde's view, progress is always eschatological in nature. One is not being transformed morally into the image of Christ. Rather, the eschatological reality of perfect sanctification breaks into the present. In Forde's words, the "progress Luther has in mind is not our movement toward the goal but the goal's movement in on us."[41] This difference is further rooted in Forde's disagreements with Aristotle. Following the ancient philosopher, the Lutheran scholastics contended that there is a difference between a thing's substance and its accidental qualities. The substance defines what a thing is, and the accidents are properties of that thing which can be subject to change. For the scholastics, there is a continual human substance which remains consistent from the unregenerate to regenerate state, which remains with the individual throughout eternity. Both the impacts of sin and sanctification are accidental in nature, rather than substantive. In other words, the human subject retains the same identity both before and after conversion. For Forde, this disrupts the eschatological nature of the gospel, wherein the creature is made *completely* new. There is no moral improvement in the accidental sense then, but only in terms of one being made a totally new creation. The problem with such an approach is that negates redemption altogether and promotes a Flacian understanding of sin. If there is only discontinuity between the old and new, then one cannot speak of redemption in any coherent sense whatsoever. The human nature itself must be destroyed and replaced by a new person, rather than a sinful creature receiving redemption while simultaneously retaining his own identity. The utilization of the categories of substance and accident (which is affirmed in FC SD I.55) is not simply an imposition of pagan philosophical ideas onto Christian theology, but it helps to maintain two biblical truths. First, one is profoundly impacted by sin and is profoundly changed by the gospel. Second, the human creature retains his essential identity as a good creation of God even after the fall, and this identity is retained in the act of redemption.

A more consistently confessional approach to the *simul iustus et peccator* principle in relation to the ethical life is explained by Gilbert

---

41. Braaten, *Christian Dogmatics* 2:435.

Meilaender in his volume *The Theory and Practice of Virtue*. Meilaender, a member of the LCMS, proposes a system of virtue ethics through the ancient philosophical traditions of Plato and Aristotle and more modern ethicists such as Josef Pieper and Alasdair MacIntyre. In his view, such an approach to ethics is perfectly consistent with traditional Lutheran theology. As a Lutheran, Meilaender addresses the question of virtue in relation to Luther's central doctrine of justification. He affirms, like the historic Lutheran tradition, that in one sense there is no need for personal virtue at all, because Christ's own merit is imputed to the sinner by faith. Lutheran piety often emphasizes one's lack of personal virtue, and the necessity of receiving the virtue of Christ as a divine gift. In summary, Luther emphasizes being (justification) over doing (sanctification).[42] One might (wrongly) conclude from this that virtue ethics are completely incompatible with Luther's own thought. Steven Paulson does this through his consistently negative statements about virtue, arguing that the Christian faith puts an end to the search for virtue altogether. Virtue is the essence of the human problem, rather than a goal which is to be obtained through the help of God.[43] Kilcrease is similarly critical of virtue ethics as a Lutheran model in his review of Biermann's writing. But Meilaender demonstrates that virtue *is* consistent with Luther's own thought.

Like Forde, Meilaender argues that Luther can speak of *simul iustus et peccator* in two divergent manners. At times, Luther refers to this reality in reference to total states, and in other places, this refers to two partial realities. One is both totally saint–totally sinner, and part saint–part sinner. The solution Meilaender offers differs from that of Forde and is more consistent with the Lutheran tradition and biblical witness. He demonstrates that Luther holds both of these ideas together consistently in his treatise *Against Latomus*, wherein he makes the distinction between Christ as the favor and *donum* of God. In the first instance, God judges not merely the deeds of an individual, but the whole person. If one is outside of Christ, that individual is judged a sinner. If one is in Christ, one is judged a saint. The Christian therefore is declared both righteous (in Christ) and sinful (in his own righteousness). This is not the only manner in which Luther speaks about righteousness, however. Luther consistently speaks about progress in the Christian life, wherein one travels on a path from sinner to saint. It is in this sense that one can genuinely utilize language of virtue as one develops

---

42. Meilaender, *Virtue Ethics*, 107.
43. Paulson, *Lutheran Theology*, 2.

Conclusion

the moral life. This is not a pure moralistic enterprise, as it is the grace of regeneration which aids one in the virtuous life. Regeneration serves as the basis and foundation of moral living, and God's grace sustains and guides one in this enterprise. Meilaender makes a distinction here between a "substantive" and "relational" understanding of virtue.[44] In a substantive sense, one is constantly progressing in the moral life, as an individual experiences actual change. Relationally, however, there is no progress. One is either in a positive relationship to God through faith or not. These two concepts are held together in tension in Luther's thought, as the truth of justification by faith and the necessity of the moral life are affirmed.

This distinction made by Meilaender between the substantive and relational aspects of the moral life are similar to the more recently studied distinction between active and passive righteousness. Biermann's further work on virtue ethics offers a more nuanced and consistent approach to the relationship of the justified believer and Christian ethics. In his treatment of the subject, Biermann proposes that virtue is a proper and essential category for Lutheran theologians that is addressed in the writings of Luther and the confessional documents. The exposition of virtue is not, then, a departure from the Lutheran tradition, but is inherent within older writers. With Elert and existential Lutheranism, such ethical discussions gradually disappeared from the Lutheran landscape, but this is an oddity within Lutheran history rather than the norm. Significantly, Biermann points out that in the Apology of the Augsburg Confession, Melanchthon admits that no one has written more eloquently about civic virtue than Aristotle (Apol AC IV.14). The problem with virtue, for Melanchthon, Luther, and other early Reformers, is that it is often confused with justifying righteousness, and thereby denies the efficacy of faith as the sole means of justification. The solution Biermann offers is not to just jettison talk of specific ethical questions from the theological task altogether, as Forde and Paulson do, but to distinguish between two different kinds of righteousness.

The two kinds of righteousness defined by Biermann, as well as in texts cited above from Charles Arand, is a means whereby the theologian is able to distinguish between two different realms in which everyone lives, and the divergent types of righteousness that correspond to each. *Coram Deo*, one lives solely by passive righteousness. In this realm, Forde is correct that virtue is irrelevant to the life of faith. There is no virtue or moral improvement which effects this righteousness, which is purely a divine gift.

---

44. Meilaender, *Virtue Ethics*, 119.

This corresponds to the relational aspect of the ethical life as explained by Meilaender. Righteousness *coram Deo* is about the status of one's relation to God, which is not measured through partial realities. Justification is total and complete, just as the guilty ruling against sin is total and complete. In this realm, the Christian is *totus-iustus, totus-peccator*. In relation to the broader world, however, one is in the process of gradual moral improvement. This is the realm of Christian sanctification. It is in this sense that the "substantive righteousness" explained by Meilaender is a partial and growing reality within the individual. Here, one is *partim-iustus, partim-peccator*. Biermann refers to this as "conforming righteousness," wherein one is gradually conformed to the image of God through the cultivation of virtue.[45] This distinction is essential, because it assures that one can speak of the virtuous life without fear that it will somehow distort one's view of justification. Forde's fears about the moral life impacting the eschatological nature of justification are unfounded if this distinction is properly understood. In a two-kinds-of-righteousness framework, justification and sanctification are placed into two distinctive realms, so that one is not taught at the expense of the other. This guards against moralistic interpretations of the Christian faith which mitigate the centrality of justification by faith, as well as the law-gospel reductionism of Gerhard Forde.

The division between Gerhard Forde and the confessional Lutheran tradition surrounding ethics and morality has immensely practical implications. These divergent perspectives significantly alter the role and function of the pastoral office. For Forde, the pastor's role is simply to deliver the law and the gospel to his hearers in the context of primary theological discourse. The delivery of the gospel in this context kills the old and raises the new person to life. Good deeds then flow spontaneously through the individual who has participated in this death and resurrection. Ethical instruction is then not a central aspect of the pastoral office, or of the church in general. In the confessional approach to the Christian life, the continual declaration of justification *sola fide* and the necessity of the ethical life coexist. The church has a duty both to freely proclaim law and gospel, and thereby justify sinners, and to speak to the moral and ethical issues addressed in Scripture. The manner in which these two realities exist alongside one another is best explained through the distinction between the two kinds of righteousness. *Coram Deo*, one is righteous through the

---

45. Ibid., 149.

CONCLUSION

alien righteousness of Christ. *Coram mundo*, one is shaped by the Spirit through the cultivation of virtue.

Further Areas of Study

Gerhard Forde's theological revision is extensive in nature, and thus an entire explication of the areas in which his theological convictions diverge from the historic Lutheran tradition is impossible in a study of this size. In this treatment, Forde's perspective on law and gospel in particular has been evaluated. While other areas of theology, ethics, and philosophy have been addressed, this has only been done insofar as these ideas directly relate to the distinction between law and gospel. Several other areas can and should be explored in future studies on the topic.

One of the most important aspects of Forde's thought is his underlying philosophical convictions. Here, the general idea that act has priority over being has been explained, especially in relation to the definition of God's law. Further study is merited on the various implications of such a conviction, not only in the thought of Forde himself, but also in the writings of others who are in the broader Radical Lutheran tradition. Forde is not alone in his rejection of traditional metaphysics; a number of writers have argued against what is viewed as a Greek imposition on Lutheran thought. Oswald Bayer has argued that Luther's theological revolution was largely a hermeneutical one, and he has purported that rather than ontology, Lutheran thought emphasizes linguistic philosophy. Therefore, things should not be defined in terms of their essence, but in connection with their existence through God's speech-act. These ideas have influenced other writers such as Steven Paulson and Mark Mattes, who similarly speak with skepticism about traditional metaphysical categories. From the confessional Lutheran tradition, some writers such as Robert Kolb and William Schumacher have also argued for a linguistic perspective of reality. These contemporary developments have not generally been studied in connection with the traditional metaphysical system as found in Johann Gerhard and the Lutheran confessions. Such a study needs to be done in order to compare and contrast these various differences in order that the compatibility between contemporary movements and the historic views might be explored.

These underlying metaphysical views lead to a number of different revisions of Christian theology. While this study explored the doctrine of the law in particular, some other even more significant areas are affected. The most notable of these is the doctrine of God. The Lutheran scholastics function on the same convictions as the medieval scholastics with regard to the doctrine of God. There is no significant departure from Thomas Aquinas surrounding the existence and attributes of divinity. In the nineteenth century, Lutheran theologians began to depart from more traditional approaches to God's being. Isaak Dorner purports that the Reformation truths discovered in the sixteenth century were never sufficiently applied to the doctrine of God. In an attempt to formulate an evangelical view of God, Dorner neglected the traditional doctrine of divine immutability. Other theologians, such as Hofmann and Martensen, were influenced by the philosophy of idealism and included God within a historical process. Forde and other Radical Lutherans are thus not alone in their rejection of traditional categories of divinity within Lutheran thought. This is not even their primary concern in the explication of theology. However, they do promote their own particular views of divinity which differ from both the confessional Lutheran tradition and earlier Lutheran theological revisions of traditional dogma. The division between law and gospel as promoted by Forde leads to a God who contradicts himself, or who "becomes other" as the gospel triumphs over the law within his own being. Further, the prioritization of act over being leads to a description of God himself as act (not in the traditional sense of *actus purus*). These ideas merit their own future study in which this view of God is compared with that of the Lutheran scholastics and the compatibility of these two perspectives is explored.

Conclusion

Radical Lutheranism as defended by Gerhard Forde and the confessional Lutheran approach as explicated by the Protestant scholastics present alternative and contradictory approaches to the distinction between law and gospel. The ideas of the two systems cannot be reconciled. While they agree on the basic idea that the law and the gospel should be distinguished from one another, and that they have different effects upon the human creature, they differ on the precise definition of both the law and the gospel. These differences are not mere minutiae in the dogmatic expositions of the two topics but are at the center of each system. For Forde, the law is not the eternal will of God, but is a phrase which refers to the existential impact of a hidden God of wrath upon the sinner. For the orthodox, the law is

Conclusion

the eternal and immutable will of God which is revealed through his commandments. For Forde, the gospel is defined by its act upon the sinner, wherein one is brought into the new age through the death-resurrection act of justification. For the scholastics, the gospel is an objective reality that is founded upon the active and passive obedience of Christ, which is then imparted to the sinner through forensic justification. One simply cannot reconcile these two ideas, and these are, at heart, two different theological traditions entirely.

Bibliography

Arand, Charles P. "Two Kinds of Righteousness as a Framework for Law and Gospel in the Apology." *Concordia Journal* 33/2 (2001) 417–39.
Arand, Charles P. and Joel Biermann. "Why the Two Kinds of Righteousness?" *Concordia Journal* 33/2 (2007) 116–35.
Arand, Charles P., Robert Kolb and James A. Nestingen. *The Lutheran Confessions: A History and Theology of the Book of Concord*. Minneapolis: Fortress, 2012.
Ashmon, Scott A. "Revisiting the Law-Gospel Paradigm in Light of the Old Testament." *Concordia Pulpit Resources* 26/3 (2016) 3–8.
Aulen, Gustav. *Christus Victor: An Historical Study of the Three Main Types of the Idea of the Atonement*. Translated by A. G. Herbert. London: SPCK, 1931.
Barth, Karl. *The Word of God and the Word of Man*. Translated by D. Horton. New York: Harper & Row, 1957.
Bayer, Oswald. *Living by Faith: Justification and Sanctification*. Translated by Geoffrey Bromily. Grand Rapids: Eerdmans, 2007.
———. *Theology the Lutheran Way*. Translated by Jeffrey Silcock and Mark Mattes. Grand Rapids: Eerdmans, 2007.
Becker, Matthew L. *The Self-Giving God and Salvation History: The Trinitarian Theology of Johannes von Hofmann*. New York: T&T, 2004.
Bente, F. Translator. *Triglot Concordia: The Symbolical Books of the Ev. Lutheran Church*. St. Louis: Concordia, 1921.
Biermann, Joel D. *A Case for Character: Towards a Lutheran Virtue Ethics*. Minneapolis: Fortress, 2014.
Braaten, Carl E. and Robert W. Jenson. *Christian Dogmatics*. Philadelphia: Fortress, 1984.
Bradley, John and Robert Muller. *Church History: An Introduction to Research, Reference Works, and Methods*. Grand Rapids: Eerdmans, 1995.
Bultmann, Rudolph. *The Presence of Eternity: History and Eschatology*. New York: Harper, 1962.
Cary, Phillip. "*Sola Fide*: Luther and Calvin." *Concordia Theological Quarterly* 71 1/2 (2009) 265–81.
Chemnitz, Martin. *Examination of the Council of Trent*. Vol. 1. Translated by Fred Kramer. St. Louis: Concordia, 1971.
———. *Loci Theologici*. Translated by J.A.O. Preus. St. Louis: Concordia, 1989.

Bibliography

Clark, R. Scott. *Recovering the Reformed Confession: Our Theology, Piety, and Practice.* Phillipsburg, NJ: P&R, 2008.

Cooper, Jordan. *Hands of Faith: A Historical and Theological Study of the Two Kinds of Righteousness in Lutheran Thought.* Eugene, OR: Wipf and Stock, 2016.

———. *The Great Divide: A Lutheran Evaluation of Reformed Theology.* Eugene, OR: Wipf and Stock, 2015.

Dunn, J. D. G. *The New Perspective on Paul.* Grand Rapids: Eerdmans, 2007.

Elert, Werner. *The Structure of Lutheranism.* Translated by Walter A. Hansen. St. Louis: Concordia, 1962.

Forde, Gerhard O. *The Law-Gospel Debate: An Interpretation of Its Historical Development.* Minneapolis: Fortress, 1969.

———. *Where God Meets Man: Luther's Down-to-Earth Approach to the Gospel.* Minneapolis: Augsburg, 1972.

———. *Justification by Faith: A Matter of Life and Death.* Mifflintown, PA: Sigler, 1990.

———. *Theology Is for Proclamation.* Fortress: Minneapolis, 1990.

———. *On Being a Theologian of the Cross: Reflections on Luther's Heidelberg Disputation, 1518.* Grand Rapids: Eerdmans, 1997.

———. *A More Radical Gospel: Essays on Eschatology, Authority, Atonement, and Ecumenism.* Edited by M. C. Mattes and S. D. Paulson. Grand Rapids: Eerdmans, 2004.

———. *The Captivation of the Will: Luther v. Erasmus on Freedom and Bondage.* Grand Rapids: Eerdmans, 2005.

———. *The Preached God: Proclamation in Word and Sacrament.* Edited by M. C. Mattes and S. D. Paulson. Grand Rapids: Eerdmans, 2007.

Frame, John R. "Law and Gospel." *Frame-Poythress*, 2012. www.Frame-Poythress.org/law-and-gospel/

———. *Systematic Theology.* Phillipsburg, NJ: P&R, 2013.

Frtiz, John H. *Pastoral Theology: A Handbook of Scriptural Principles Written Especially for Pastors of the Lutheran Church.* St. Louis: Concordia, 1932.

Gaffin, Richard B., Jr. *By Faith, Not by Sight: Paul and the Order of Salvation.* 2nd ed. Philipsburg, NJ: P&R, 2013.

———. *Resurrection and Redemption: A Study in Paul's Soteriology.* 2nd ed. Phillipsburg, NJ: P&R, 1987.

Gerberding, George Henry. *The Lutheran Pastor.* Philadelphia: Lutheran Publication Society, 1902.

Gerhard, Johann. *On the Law of God and On the Ceremonial and Forensic Laws.* Translated by Richard J. Dinda. St. Louis: Concordia, 2015.

Gieschen, Charles A. *The Law in Holy Scripture: Essays from the Concordia Theological Seminary Symposium.* St. Louis: Concordia, 2004.

Grimenstein, Edward O. *A Lutheran Primer for Preaching.* St. Louis: Concordia, 2015.

Gritsch, Eric W. *A History of Lutheranism.* Minneapolis: Fortress, 2002.

Grobien, Gifford. "Righteousness, Mystical Union, and Moral Formation in Christian Worship." *Concordia Theological Quarterly* 77/1–2 (2013) 141–64.

Hesselink, John. "Law and Gospel or Gospel and Law? Karl Barth, Martin Luther, and John Calvin." *Reformation and Revival* 14/1 (2005) 139–171.

Horton, Michael Scott. *The Christian Faith: A Systematic Theology of the Christian Faith.* Grand Rapids: Zondervan, 2011.

Iwand, Hans J. *The Righteousness of Faith According to Luther.* Translated by R. H. Lundell. Eugene, OR: Wipf and Stock, 2008.

Bibliography

Jacobs, Henry Eyster. *A Summary of the Christian Faith.* Philadelphia: General Council, 1907.

———. 1913. *Elements of Religion.* Philadelphia: General Council, 1913.

Jenson, Robert W. *Systematic Theology: The Triune God.* Oxford: Oxford, 1997.

Kilcrease, Jack D. "Gerhard Forde's Doctrine of the Law: A Confessional Lutheran Critique." *Concordia Theological Quarterly* 75/1-2 (2011) 151-79.

———. "Gerhard Forde's Theology of Atonement and Justification: A Confessional Lutheran Response." *Concordia Theological Quarterly* 76/3-4 (2012) 269-93.

———. "Review Essay: *A Case for Character: Toward a Lutheran Virtue Ethics.*" *Logia: A Journal of Lutheran Theology* 24/4 (2015) 49-51.

Kolb, Robert, and Timothy J. Wengert, eds. *The Book of Concord: The Confessions of the Evangelical Lutheran Church.* Translated by C. Arand, et. al. Minneapolis: Fortress, 2000.

Kolb, Robert and Charles P. Arand. *The Genius of Luther's Theology: A Wittenberg Way of Thinking for the Contemporary Church.* Grand Rapids: Baker, 2008.

Lindberg, Conrad E. *Christian Dogmatics and Notes on the History of Dogma.* Rock Island, IL: Augustana, 1922.

Lindberg, Duane. *To Tell the Truth: A History of the AALC 1987-2012.* Fort Wayne, IN: TAALC, 2014.

Lotz, David W. *Ritschl and Luther: A Fresh Perspective on Albrecht Ritschl's Theology in Light of His Luther Study.* Nashville: Abingdon, 1974.

Macquarrie, John. *An Existentialist Theology: A Comparison of Heidegger and Bultmann.* New York: Harper, 2006.

Martensen, Hans. *Christian Dogmatics.* Edinburgh: T&T Clark, 1898.

Marquart, Kurt E. *The Saving Truth: Doctrine for Laypeople.* St. Louis: Luther Academy, 2016.

Mattes, Mark C. *The Role of Justification in Contemporary Theology.* Grand Rapids: Eerdmans, 2004.

Meyers, Carl S. *Moving Frontiers: Readings in the History of the Lutheran Church Missouri Synod.* St. Louis: Concordia, 1986.

Mildenberger, Friedrich. *Theology of the Lutheran Confessions.* Translated by E. Lueker. Philadelphia: Fortress, 1986.

Murray, Scott R. *Law, Life, and the Living God: The Third Use of the Law in Modern American Lutheranism.* Saint Louis: Concordia, 2001.

Nakskow, Petrus S. *Articles of Faith of the Holy Evangelical Church According to the Word of God and the Augsburg Confession Set Forth in Forty Sermons.* Translated by J. M. Magens. New York: Parker and Wyman, 1754.

Oliphant, Scott K., ed. *Justified in Christ: God's Plan for Us in Justification.* London: Mentor, 2001.

Paulson, Steven D. *Lutheran Theology.* New York: T&T Clark, 2011.

Pieper, Franz. *Christian Dogmatics.* 4 Vols. Saint Louis: Concordia, 1950-1957.

Piper, John. *Counted Righteous in Christ: Should We Abandon the Imputation of Christ's Righteousness?* Wheaton, IL: Crossway, 2002.

Preus, Robert D. *A Contemporary Look at the Formula of Concord.* St. Louis: Concordia, 1978.

Sanders, E. P. *Paul and Palestinian Judaism: A Comparison of Patterns of Religion.* Philadelphia, Fortress, 1977.

Bibliography

Sandlin, Andrew P. *Wrongly Dividing the Word: Overcoming the Law-Gospel Distinction.* Mount Hermon, CA: Kerygma Press, 2007.

Sasse, Herman. *We Confess the Sacraments.* Translated by N. Nagel. St. Louis: Concordia, 1985.

Scaer, David P. "Finding a Place for the Third Use of the Law in Our Preaching." *Concordia Pulpit Resources* 25/1 (2016) 3–9.

———. *Law and Gospel and the Means of Grace.* St. Louis: Luther Academy, 2008.

Schlink, Edmund. *Theology of the Lutheran Confessions.* Translated by P. F. Koehneke. Saint Louis: Concordia, 1961.

Schmid, Heinrich. *The Doctrinal Theology of the Evangelical Lutheran Church.* Translated by Charles A. Hay and Henry Eyster Jacobs. Minneapolis: Augsburg, 1875.

Smith, K. G. *Academic Writing and Theological Research: A Guide for Students.* Johannesburg: South African Theological Seminary, 2008.

Stendahl, Krister. *Paul Among Jews and Gentiles, and Other Essays.* Philadelphia: Fortress, 1976.

Stump, Joseph. *The Christian Faith: A System of Christian Dogmatics.* Philadelphia: Muhlenberg, 1942.

Suelflow, August R. *Servant of the Word: The Life and Ministry of C.F.W. Walther.* St. Louis: Concordia, 2000.

Tipton, Lane S. "Union with Christ and Justification." In *Justified in Christ: God's Plan for Us in Justification*, edited by K. Scott Oliphant, 23–50. London: Mentor, 2007.

Vickers, Brian. *Jesus' Blood and Righteousness: Paul's Theology of Imputation.* Wheaton, IL: Crossway, 2006.

Voigt, Andrew G. *Biblical Dogmatics.* Columbia, SC: Lutheran Board of Publication, 1917.

Vlachos, Chris A. *The Law and the Knowledge of Good and Evil: The Edenic Background of the Catalytic Operation of the Law in Paul.* Eugene, OR: Pickwick, 2009.

Walther, C. F. W. *From Our Master's Table.* Translated by Joel R. Baseley. Dearborn, MI: Mark V, 2008.

———. *Pastoral Theology.* Translated by J. M. Drickamer. St. Louis: Concordia, 1995.

Weidner, R. F. *Biblical Theology of the Old Testament.* Rock Island, IL: Augustana, 1896.

———. *Christian Ethics: A System Based on Martensen and Harless.* New York: Flemming H. Revel, 1891.

———. *Pneumatology: Or the Doctrine Concerning the Holy Spirit.* Chicago: Wartburg, 1915.

Westerholm, Stephen. *Perspectives Old and New on Paul: The "Lutheran" Paul and His Critics.* Grand Rapids, MI, 2004.

Wingren, Gustaf. *Creation and Law.* Translated by R. MacKenzie. Eugene, OR: Wipf and Stock, 2003.

———. *Luther on Vocation.* Translated by C. C. Rasmussen. Philadelphia: Muhlenberg, 1957.

Wright, N. T. *What St. Paul Really Said: Was Paul of Tarsus the Real Founder of Christianity?* Grand Rapids: Eerdmans, 1997.

Yaghjian, L. B. *Writing Theology Well: A Rhetoric for Theological and Biblical Writers.* New York: Continuum, 2006.

Yeago, David S. "Gnosticism, Antinomianism, and Reformation Theology: Reflections on the Costs of a Construal." *Pro Ecclesia.* 2/1 (1993) 38–39.

Zimmerman, Paul A. *A Seminary in Crisis: The Inside Story of the Preus Fact Finding Committee.* St. Louis: Concordia, 2007.

www.ingramcontent.com/pod-product-compliance
Lightning Source LLC
Chambersburg PA
CBHW071507150426
43191CB00009B/1441